SELECTED POEMS

WALTER
DE LA MARE

Selected Poems

Chosen by
R. N. Green-Armytage

faber and faber
LONDON · BOSTON

This selection of poems
first published in 1954
by Faber and Faber Limited
3 Queen Square London WC1N 3AU
First published in Faber Paperbacks 1973

Printed and bound in Great Britain by
Mackays of Chatham PLC, Chatham, Kent

ISBN 0 571 10401 0

7 9 10 8

This Selection
of Walter de la Mare's Poems
is Dedicated to
his eleven grand-children

NICOLAS, SHIRLEY, ALBINIA, GILES,
STEPHEN, RICHARD, BENEDICK, JULIAN,
JULIA, CHARMIAN, AND MICHAEL

Inter spem curamque, timores inter et iras
Omnem crede diem tibi diluxisse supremum;
Grata superveniet, quae non sperabitur, hora.
HORACE, Ep. I, iv

R.N.G—A.

CONTENTS

I

POEMS (1906)

II

THE LISTENERS (1912)

III

MOTLEY (1918)

IV

THE VEIL (1921)

V

THE FLEETING (1933)

VI

MEMORY (1938)

VII

THE BURNING GLASS (1945)

VIII

INWARD COMPANION (1950)

IX

THE TRAVELLER (1945)   *page* 151

X

O LOVELY ENGLAND (1953)

XI

RHYMES AND VERSES

THE HAPPY ENCOUNTER

I saw sweet Poetry turn troubled eyes
   On shaggy Science nosing in the grass,
   For by that way poor Poetry must pass
On her long pilgrimage to Paradise.
He snuffled, grunted, squealed; perplexed by flies,
   Parched, weatherworn, and near of sight, alas,
   From peering close where very little was
In dens secluded from the open skies.

But Poetry in bravery went down,
   And called his name, soft, clear, and fearlessly;
Stooped low, and stroked his muzzle overgrown;
   Refreshed his drought with dew; wiped pure and free
   His eyes: and lo! laughed loud for joy to see
In those grey deeps the azure of her own.

SHADOW

Even the beauty of the rose doth cast,
When its bright, fervid noon is past,
A still and lengthening shadow in the dust
    Till darkness come
    And take its strange dream home.

The transient bubbles of the water paint
'Neath their frail arch a shadow faint;
The golden nimbus of the windowed saint,
    Till shine the stars,
    Casts pale and trembling bars.

The loveliest thing earth hath, a shadow hath,
A dark and livelong hint of death,
Haunting it ever till its last faint breath. . .
    Who, then, may tell
The beauty of heaven's shadowless asphodel?

THE BIRTHNIGHT: TO F.

Dearest, it was a night
That in its darkness rocked Orion's stars;
A sighing wind ran faintly white
Along the willows, and the cedar boughs
Laid their wide hands in stealthy peace across
The starry silence of their antique moss:
No sound save rushing air
Cold, yet all sweet with Spring,
And in thy mother's arms, couched weeping there,
    Thou, lovely thing.

SEA-MAGIC

My heart faints in me for the distant sea.
  The roar of London is the roar of ire
  The lion utters in his old desire
For Libya out of dim captivity.

The long bright silver of Cheapside I see,
  Her gilded weathercocks on roof and spire
  Exulting eastward in the western fire;
All things recall one heart-sick memory:—

Ever the rustle of the advancing foam,
  The surges' desolate thunder, and the cry
  As of some lone babe in the whispering sky;
Ever I peer into the restless gloom
  To where a ship clad dim and loftily
Looms steadfast in the wonder of her home.

NAPOLEON

'What is the world, O soldiers?
      It is I:
  I, this incessant snow,
      This northern sky;
  Soldiers, this soltitude
      Through which we go
          Is I.'

EVEN IN THE GRAVE

I laid my inventory at the hand
    Of Death, who in his gloomy arbour sate;
    And while he conned it, sweet and desolate
I heard Love singing in that quiet land.
He read the record even to the end—
    The heedless, livelong injuries of Fate,
    The burden of foe, the burden of love and hate;
The wounds of foe, the bitter wounds of friend:

All, all, he read, ay, even the indifference,
    The vain talk, vainer silence, hope and dream.
He questioned me: 'What seek'st thou then instead'?
    I bowed my face in the pale evening gleam.
Then gazed he on me with strange innocence:
    'Even in the grave thou wilt have thyself,' he said.

THEY TOLD ME

They told me Pan was dead, but I
    Oft marvelled who it was that sang
Down the green valleys languidly
    Where the grey elder-thickets hang.

Sometimes I thought it was a bird
    My soul had charged with sorcery;
Sometimes it seemed my own heart heard
    Inland the sorrow of the sea.

But even where the primrose sets
    The seal of her pale loveliness,
I found amid the violets
    Tears of an antique bitterness.

MERCUTIO

Along an avenue of almond-trees
Came three girls chattering of their sweethearts three
And lo! Mercutio, with Byronic ease,
Out of his philosophic eye cast all
A mere flowered twig of thought, whereat—
Three hearts fell still as when an air dies out
And Venus falters lonely o'er the sea.
But when within the furthest mist of bloom
His step and form were hid, the smooth child Ann
Said, 'La, and what eyes he had!' and Lucy said,
'How sad a gentleman!' and Katherine,
'I wonder, now, what mischief he was at.'
And these three also April hid away,
Leaving the Spring faint with Mercutio.

AUTUMN

There is wind where the rose was;
Cold rain where sweet grass was;
　　And clouds like sheep
　　Stream o'er the steep
Grey skies where the lark was.

Nought gold where your hair was;
Nought warm where your hand was;
　　But phantom, forlorn,
　　Beneath the thorn,
Your ghost where your face was.

Sad winds where your voice was;
Tears, tears where my heart was;
　　And ever with me,
　　Child, ever with me,
Silence where hope was.

KEEP INNOCENCY

Like an old battle, youth is wild
With bugle and spear, and counter cry,
Fanfare and drummery, yet a child
Dreaming of that sweet chivalry,
The piercing terror cannot see.

He, with a mild and serious eye,
Along the azure of the years,
Sees the sweet pomp sweep hurtling by;
But he sees not death's blood and tears,
Sees not the plunging of the spears.

And all the strident horror of
Horse and rider, in red defeat,
Is only music fine enough
To lull him into slumber sweet
In fields where ewe and lambkin bleat.

O, if with such simplicity
Himself take arms and suffer war;
With beams his targe shall gilded be,
Though in the thickening gloom be far
The steadfast light of any star!

Though hoarse War's eagle on him perch,
Quickened with guilty lightnings—there
It shall in vain for terror search,
Where a child's eyes 'neath bloody hair
Gaze purely through the dingy air.

And when the wheeling rout is spent,
Though in the heaps of slain he lie,
Or lonely in his last content;
Quenchless shall burn in secrecy
The flame Death knows his victors by.

REMEMBRANCE

The sky was like a waterdrop
  In shadow of a thorn,
Clear, tranquil, beautiful,
  Dark, forlorn.

Lightning along its margin ran;
  A rumour of the sea
Rose in profundity and sank
  Into infinity.

Lofty and few the elms, the stars
  In the vast boughs most bright;
I stood a dreamer in a dream
  In the unstirring night.

Not wonder, worship, not even peace
  Seemed in my heart to be:
Only the memory of one,
  Of all most dead to me.

TO MY MOTHER

Thine is my all, how little when 'tis told
      Beside thy gold!
Thine the first peace, and mine the livelong strife;
Thine the clear dawn, and mine the night of life;
      Thine the unstained belief,
      Darkened in grief.

Scarce even a flower but thine its beauty and name,
      Dimmed, yet the same;
Never in twilight comes the moon to me,
Stealing thro' those far woods, but tells of thee,
      Falls, dear, on my wild heart,
      And takes thy part.

Thou art the child, and I—how steeped in age!
      A blotted page
From that clear, little book life's taken away:
How could I read it, dear, so dark the day?
      Be it all memory
      'Twixt thee and me!

ENGLAND

No lovelier hills than thine have laid
   My tired thoughts to rest:
No peace of lovelier valleys made
   Like peace within my breast.

Thine are the woods whereto my soul,
   Out of the noontide beam,
Flees for a refuge green and cool
   And tranquil as a dream.

Thy breaking seas like trumpets peal;
   Thy clouds—how oft have I
Watched their bright towers of silence steal
   Into infinity!

My heart within me faints to roam
   In thought even far from thee:
Thine be the grave whereto I come,
   And thine my darkness be.

THE THREE CHERRY TREES

There were three cherry trees once,
　Grew in a garden all shady;
And there for delight of so gladsome a sight,
　Walked a most beautiful lady,
　Dreamed a most beautiful lady.

Birds in those branches did sing,
　Blackbird and throstle and linnet,
But she walking there was by far the most fair—
　Lovelier than all else within it,
　Blackbird and throstle and linnet.

But blossoms to berries do come,
　All hanging on stalks light and slender,
And one long summer's day charmed that lady away,
　With vows sweet and merry and tender;
　A lover with voice low and tender.

Moss and lichen the green branches deck;
　Weeds nod in its paths green and shady:
Yet a light footstep seems there to wander in dreams,
　The ghost of that beautiful lady,
　That happy and beautiful lady.

NIGHT

That shining moon—watched by that one faint star:
Sure now am I, beyond the fear of change,
The lovely in life is the familiar,
And only the lovelier for continuing strange.

THE SCARECROW

All winter through I bow my head
  Beneath the driving rain;
The North Wind powders me with snow
  And blows me black again;
At midnight in a maze of stars
  I flame with glittering rime,
And stand, above the stubble, stiff
  As mail at morning-prime.
But when that child, called Spring, and all
  His host of children, come,
Scattering their buds and dew upon
  These acres of my home,
Some rapture in my rags awakes;
  I lift void eyes and scan
The skies for crows, those ravening foes,
  Of my strange master, Man.
I watch him striding lank behind
  His clashing team, and know
Soon will the wheat swish body high
  Where once lay sterile snow;
Soon shall I gaze across a sea
  Of sun-begotten grain,
Which my unflinching watch hath sealed
  For harvest once again.

MARTHA

'Once . . . once upon a time . . .'
  Over and over again,
Martha would tell us her stories,
  In the hazel glen.

Hers were those clear grey eyes
  You watch, and the story seems
Told by their beautifulness
  Tranquil as dreams.

She'd sit with her two slim hands
  Clasped round her bended knees;
While we on our elbows lolled,
  And stared at ease.

Her voice and her narrow chin,
  Her grave small lovely head,
Seemed half the meaning
  Of the words she said.

'Once . . . once upon a time . . .'
  Like a dream you dream in the night,
Fairies and gnomes stole out
  In the leaf-green light.

And her beauty far away
  Would fade, as her voice ran on,
Till hazel and summer sun
  And all were gone:

All fordone and forgot;
  And like clouds in the height of the sky,
Our hearts stood still in the hush
  Of an age gone by.

NOD

Softly along the road of evening,
  In a twilight dim with rose,
Wrinkled with age, and drenched with dew,
  Old Nod, the shepherd, goes.

His drowsy flock streams on before him,
  Their fleeces charged with gold,
To where the sun's last beam leans low
  On Nod the shepherd's fold.

The hedge is quick and green with brier,
  From their sand the conies creep;
And all the birds that fly in heaven
  Flock singing home to sleep.

His lambs outnumber a noon's roses,
  Yet when night's shadows fall,
His blind old sheep-dog, Slumber-soon,
  Misses not one of all.

His are the quiet steeps of dreamland,
  The waters of no-more-pain,
His ram's bell rings 'neath an arch of stars,
  'Rest, rest, and rest again.'

DREAMS

Be gentle, O hands of a child;
Be true: like a shadowy sea
In the starry darkness of night
    Are your eyes to me.

But words are shallow, and soon
Dreams fade that the heart once knew;
And youth fades out in the mind,
    In the dark eyes too.

What can a tired heart say,
Which the wise of the world have made dumb?
Save to the lonely dreams of a child,
    'Return again, come!'

BE ANGRY NOW NO MORE

Be angry now no more!
    If I have grieved thee—if
Thy kindness, mine before,
No hope may now restore:
    Only forgive, forgive!

If still resentment burns
    In thy cold breast, oh, if
No more to pity turns,
No more, once tender, yearns
    Thy love; oh, yet forgive! . . .

Ask of the winter rain
June's withered rose again:
Ask grace of the salt sea:
She will not answer thee.
God would ten times have shriven
A heart so riven;
In her cold care thou wouldst be
Still unforgiven.

SLEEP

Men all, and birds, and creeping beasts,
  When the dark of night is deep,
From the moving wonder of their lives
  Commit themselves to sleep.

Without a thought, or fear, they shut
  The narrow gates of sense;
Heedless and quiet, in slumber turn
  Their strength to impotence.

The transient strangeness of the earth
  Their spirits no more see:
Within a silent gloom withdrawn,
  They slumber in secrecy.

Two worlds they have—a globe forgot,
  Wheeling from dark to light;
And all the enchanted realm of dream
  That burgeons out of night.

THE LISTENERS

'Is there anybody there?' said the Traveller,
  Knocking on the moonlit door;
And his horse in the silence champed the grasses
  Of the forest's ferny floor:
And a bird flew up out of the turret,
  Above the Traveller's head:
And he smote upon the door again a second time;
  'Is there anybody there?' he said.
But no one descended to the Traveller;
  No head from the leaf-fringed sill
Leaned over and looked into his grey eyes,
  Where he stood perplexed and still.
But only a host of phantom listeners
  That dwelt in the lone house then
Stood listening in the quiet of the moonlight
  To that voice from the world of men:
Stood thronging the faint moonbeams on the dark stair,
  That goes down to the empty hall,
Hearkening in an air stirred and shaken
  By the lonely Traveller's call.
And he felt in his heart their strangeness,
  Their stillness answering his cry,
While his horse moved, cropping the dark turf,
  'Neath the starred and leafy sky;
For he suddenly smote on the door, even
  Louder, and lifted his head:—
'Tell them I came, and no one answered,
  That I kept my word,' he said.
Never the least stir made the listeners,
  Though every word he spake
Fell echoing through the shadowiness of the still house
From the one man left awake:

Ay, they heard his foot upon the stirrup,
   And the sound of iron on stone,
And how the silence surged softly backward,
   When the plunging hoofs were gone.

ALL THAT'S PAST

Very old are the woods;
   And the buds that break
Out of the brier's boughs,
   When March winds wake,
So old with their beauty are—
   Oh, no man knows
Through what wild centuries
   Roves back the rose.

Very old are the brooks;
   And the rills that rise
Where snow sleeps cold beneath
   The azure skies
Sing such a history
   Of come and gone,
Their every drop is as wise
   As Solomon.

Very old are we men;
   Our dreams are tales
Told in dim Eden
   By Eve's nightingales;
We wake and whisper a while,
   But, the day gone by,
Silence and sleep like fields
   Of amaranth lie.

33

AN EPITAPH

Here lies a most beautiful lady,
Light of step and heart was she;
I think she was the most beautiful lady
That ever was in the West Country.

But beauty vanishes; beauty passes;
However rare—rare it be;
And when I crumble, who will remember
This lady of the West Country?

MUSIC UNHEARD

Sweet sounds, begone—
    Whose music on my ear
Stirs foolish discontent
    Of lingering here;
When, if I crossed
    The crystal verge of death,
Him I should see
    Who these sounds murmureth.

Sweet sounds, begone—
    Ask not my heart to break
Its bond of bravery for
    Sweet quiet's sake;
Lure not my feet
    To leave the path they must
Tread on, unfaltering,
    Till I sleep in dust.

Sweet sounds, begone!
    Though silence brings apace
Deadly disquiet
    Of this homeless place;
And all I love
    In beauty cries to me,
'We but vain shadows
    And reflections be.'

NOON AND NIGHT FLOWER

Not any flower that blows
    But shining watch doth keep;
Every swift changing chequered hour it knows
Now to break forth in beauty; now to sleep.

    This for the roving bee
    Keeps open house, and this
Stainless and clear is, that in darkness she
May lure the moth to where her nectar is.

    Lovely beyond the rest
    Are these of all delight:—
The tiny pimpernel that noon loves best,
The primrose palely burning through the night.

    One 'neath day's burning sky
    With ruby decks her place,
The other when eve's chariot glideth by
Lifts her dim torch to light that dreaming face.

HAUNTED

The rabbit in his burrow keeps
No guarded watch, in peace he sleeps;
The wolf that howls in challenging night
Cowers to her lair at morning light;
The simplest bird entwines a nest
Where she may lean her lovely breast,
Couched in the silence of the bough:—
But thou, O man, what rest hast thou?

Thy emptiest solitude can bring
Only a subtler questioning
In thy divided heart. Thy bed
Recalls at dawn what midnight said.
Seek how thou wilt to feign content,
Thy flaming ardour's quickly spent;
Soon thy last company is gone,
And leaves thee—with thyself—alone.

Pomp and great friends may hem thee round,
A thousand busy tasks be found;
Earth's thronging beauties may beguile
Thy longing lovesick heart a while;
And pride, like clouds of sunset, spread
A changing glory round thy head;
But fade will all; and thou must come,
Hating thy journey, homeless, home.

Rave how thou wilt; unmoved, remote,
That inward presence slumbers not,
Frets out each secret from thy breast
Gives thee no rally, pause, nor rest,

Scans close thy very thoughts, lest they
Should sap his patient power away;
Answers thy wrath with peace; thy cry
With tenderest taciturnity.

THE STRANGER

In the woods as I did walk,
  Dappled with the moon's beam,
I did with a Stranger talk,
  And his name was Dream.

Spurred his heel, dark his cloak,
  Shady-wide his bonnet's brim;
His horse beneath a silvery oak
  Grazed as I talked with him.

Softly his breast-brooch burned and shone;
  Hill and deep were in his eyes;
One of his hands held mine, and one
  The fruit that makes men wise.

Wondrously strange was earth to see,
  Flowers white as milk did gleam;
Spread to Heaven the Assyrian Tree,
  Over my head with Dream.

Dews were still betwixt us twain;
  Stars a trembling beauty shed;
Yet, not a whisper comes again
  Of the words he said.

SCHOLARS

Logic does well at school;
And Reason answers every question right;
Poll-parrot Memory unwinds her spool;
And Copy-cat keeps Teacher well in sight:

The Heart's a truant; nothing does by rule;
Safe in its wisdom, is taken for a fool;
Nods through the morning on the dunce's stool;
        And wakes to dream all night.

WINTER DUSK

Dark frost was in the air without,
    The dusk was still with cold and gloom,
When less than even a shadow came
    And stood within the room.

But of the three around the fire,
    None turned a questioning head to look,
Still read a clear voice, on and on,
    Still stooped they o'er their book.

The children watched their mother's eyes
    Moving on softly line to line;
It seemed to listen too—that shade,
    Yet made no outward sign.

The fire-flames crooned a tiny song,
    No cold wind stirred the wintry tree;
The children both in Faërie dreamed
    Beside their mother's knee.

And nearer yet that spirit drew
  Above that heedless one, intent
Only on what the simple words
  Of her small story meant.

No voiceless sorrow grieved her mind,
  No memory her bosom stirred,
Nor dreamed she, as she read to two,
  'Twas surely three who heard.

Yet when, the story done, she smiled
  From face to face, serene and clear,
A love, half dread, sprang up, as she
  Leaned close and drew them near.

A PRAYER

When with day's woes night haunts wake-weary eyes,
How deep a blessing from the heart may rise
On the happy, the beautiful, the good, the wise!

The poor, the outcast, knave, child, stranger, fool
Need no commending to the merciful;
But, in a world grieved, ugly, wicked, or dull,

Who could the starry influences surmise—
What praises ardent enough could prayer devise
For the happy, the beautiful, the good, the wise?

ARABIA

Far are the shades of Arabia,
  Where the Princes ride at noon,
'Mid the verdurous vales and thickets,
  Under the ghost of the moon;
And so dark is that vaulted purple
  Flowers in the forest rise
And toss into blossom 'gainst the phantom stars
  Pale in the noonday skies.

Sweet is the music of Arabia
  In my heart, when out of dreams
I still in the thin clear mirk of dawn
  Descry her gliding streams;
Hear her strange lutes on the green banks
  Ring loud with the grief and delight
Of the dim-silked, dark-haired Musicians
  In the brooding silence of night.

They haunt me—her lutes and her forests;
  No beauty on earth I see
But shadowed with that dream recalls
  Her loveliness to me:
Still eyes look coldly upon me,
  Cold voices whisper and say—
'He is crazed with the spell of far Arabia,
  They have stolen his wits away.'

NOT ONLY

Not only ruins their lichen have;
  Nor tombs alone, their moss.
Implacable Time, in markless grave,
  Turns what seemed gold to dross.

Yet—a mere ribbon for the hair,
  A broken toy, a faded flower
A passionate deathless grace may wear,
  Denied its passing hour.

THE SUNKEN GARDEN

Speak not—whisper not;
Here bloweth thyme and bergamot;
Softly on the evening hour,
Secret herbs their spices shower;
Dark-spiked rosemary and myrrh,
Lean-stalked, purple lavender;
Hides within her bosom, too,
All her sorrows, bitter rue.

Breathe not—trespass not;
Of this green and darkling spot,
Latticed from the moon's beams,
Perchance a distant dreamer dreams;
Perchance upon its darkening air,
The unseen ghosts of children fare,
Faintly swinging, sway and sweep,
Like lovely sea-flowers in the deep;
While, unmoved, to watch and ward,
Amid its gloomed and daisied sward,
Stands with bowed and dewy head
That one little leaden Lad.

THE SCRIBE

What lovely things
  Thy hand hath made:
The smooth-plumed bird
  In its emerald shade,
The seed of the grass,
  The speck of stone
Which the wayfaring ant
  Stirs—and hastes on!

Though I should sit
  By some tarn in thy hills,
Using its ink
  As the spirit wills
To write of Earth's wonders,
  Its live, willed things,
Flit would the ages
  On soundless wings
Ere unto Z
  My pen drew nigh;
Leviathan told,
  And the honey-fly:
And still would remain
  My wit to try—
My worn reeds broken,
  The dark tarn dry,
All words forgotten—
  Thou, Lord, and I.

THE LINNET

Upon this leafy bush
 With thorns and roses in it,
Flutters a thing of light,
 A twittering linnet,
And all the throbbing world
 Of dew and sun and air
By this small parcel of life
 Is made more fair:
As if each bramble-spray
 And mounded gold-wreathed furze,
Harebell and little thyme
 Were only hers;
As if this beauty and grace
 Did to one bird belong,
And, at a flutter of wing,
 Might vanish in song.

THE VACANT DAY

As I walked out in meadows green
 I heard the summer noon resound
With call of myriad things unseen
 That leapt and crept upon the ground.

High overhead the windless air
 Throbbed with the homesick coursing cry
Of swifts that ranging everwhere
 Woke echo in the sky.

44

Beside me, too, clear waters coursed
    Which willow branches, lapsing low,
Breaking their crystal gliding forced
    To sing as they did flow.

I listened; and my heart was dumb
    With praise no language could express;
Longing in vain for him to come
    Who had breathed such blessedness

On this fair world, wherein we pass
    So chequered and so brief a stay;
And yearned in spirit to learn, alas,
    What kept him still away.

MUSIC

When music sounds, gone is the earth I know,
And all her lovely things even lovelier grow;
Her flowers in vision flame, her forest trees
Lift burdened branches, stilled with ecstasies.

When music sounds, out of the water rise
Naiads whose beauty dims my waking eyes,
Rapt in strange dreams burns each enchanted face,
With solemn echoing stirs their dwelling-place.

When music sounds, all that I was I am
Ere to this haunt of brooding dust I came;
While from Time's woods break into distant song
The swift-winged hours, as I hasten along.

ALONE

The abode of the nightingale is bare,
Flowered frost congeals in the gelid air,
The fox howls from his frozen lair:
>   Alas, my loved one is gone,
>   I am alone:
>   It is winter.

Once the pink cast a winy smell,
The wild bee hung in the hyacinth bell,
Light in effulgence of beauty fell:
>   Alas, my loved one is gone,
>   I am alone:
>   It is winter.

My candle a silent fire doth shed,
Starry Orion hunts o'erhead;
Come moth, come shadow, the world is dead:
>   Alas, my loved one is gone,
>   I am alone;
>   It is winter.

THE EXILE

I am that Adam who, with Snake for guest,
Hid anguished eyes upon Eve's piteous breast.
I am that Adam who, with broken wings,
Fled from the Seraph's brazen trumpetings.
Betrayed and fugitive, I still must roam
A world where sin, and beauty, whisper of Home.

Oh, from wide circuit, shall at length I see
Pure daybreak lighten again on Eden's tree?
Loosed from remorse and hope and love's distress,
Enrobe me again in my lost nakedness?
No more with wordless grief a loved one grieve,
But to Heaven's nothingness re-welcome Eve?

THE REVENANT

O all ye fair ladies with your colours and your graces,
  And your eyes clear in flame of candle and hearth,
Toward the dark of this old window lift not up your smiling
    faces,
  Where a Shade stands forlorn from the cold of the earth.

God knows I could not rest for one I still was thinking of;
  Like a rose sheathed in beauty her spirit was to me;
Now out of unforgottenness a bitter draught I'm drinking of,
  'Tis sad of such beauty unremembered to be.

Men all are shades, O Women. Winds wist not of the way
    they blow.
  Apart from your kindness, life's at best but a snare.
Though a tongue, now past praise, this bitter thing doth say, I
    know
  What solitude means, and how, homeless, I fare.

Strange, strange, are ye all—except in beauty shared with her—
  Since I seek one I loved, yet was faithless to in death.
Not life enough I heaped, so thus my heart must fare with her,
  Now wrapt in the gross clay, bereft of life's breath.

47

VAIN QUESTIONING

What needest thou?—a few brief hours of rest
Wherein to seek thyself in thine own breast;
A transient silence wherein truth could say
Such was thy constant hope, and this thy way?—
     O burden of life that is
     A livelong tangle of perplexities!

What seekest thou?—a truce from that thou art;
Some steadfast refuge from a fickle heart;
Still to be thou, and yet no thing of scorn,
To find no stay here, and yet not forlorn?—
     O riddle of life that is
     An endless war 'twixt contrarieties.

Leave this vain questioning. Is not sweet the rose?
Sings not the wild bird ere to rest he goes?
Hath not in miracle brave June returned?
Burns not her beauty as of old it burned?
     O foolish one to roam
     So far in thine own mind away from home!

Where blooms the flower when her petals fade,
Where sleepeth echo by earth's music made,
Where all things transient to the changeless win,
There waits the peace thy spirit dwelleth in.

DUST TO DUST

Heavenly Archer, bend thy bow;
Now the flame of life burns low,
Youth is gone; I, too, would go.

Ever Fortune leads to this:
Harsh or kind, at last she is
Murderess of all ecstasies.

Yet the spirit, dark, alone,
Bound in sense, still hearkens on
For tidings of a bliss foregone.

Sleep is well for dreamless head,
At no breath astonishèd,
From the Gardens of the Dead.

I the immortal harps hear ring,
By Babylon's river languishing.
Heavenly Archer, loose thy string.

TO E.T.; 1917

You sleep too well—too far away,
    For sorrowing word to soothe or wound;
Your very quiet seems to say
    How longed-for a peace you have found.

Else, had not death so lured you on,
    You would have grieved—'twixt joy and fear—
To know how my small loving son
    Had wept for you, my dear.

THE GHOST

'Who knocks?' 'I, who was beautiful,
  Beyond all dreams to restore,
I, from the roots of the dark thorn am hither.
  And knock on the door.'

'Who speaks?' 'I—once was my speech
  Sweet as the bird's on the air,
When echo lurks by the waters to heed;
  'Tis I speak thee fair.'

'Dark is the hour!' 'Ay, and cold.'
  'Lone is my house.' 'Ah, but mine?'
'Sight, touch, lips, eyes yearned in vain.'
  'Long dead these to thine . . .'

Silence. Still faint on the porch
  Brake the flames of the stars.
In gloom groped a hope-wearied hand
  Over keys, bolts, and bars.

A face peered. All the grey night
  In chaos of vacancy shone;
Nought but vast sorrow was there
  The sweet cheat gone.

PALE-FACE

Dark are those eyes, a solemn blue:
Yes, silent Pale-face, that is true;
But I—I watch the fires that sleep
In their unfathomable deep,
Seeming a smouldering night to make
Solely for their own shining's sake.

It's common talk you're beautiful:
But I—I sometimes wonder, will
Love ever leave my judgment free
To see you as the world doth see—
'All passion spent'. No more to know
The very self that made you so.

FOR ALL THE GRIEF

For all the grief I have given with words
    May now a few clear flowers blow,
In the dust, and the heat, and the silence of birds,
    Where the friendless go.

For the thing unsaid that heart asked of me
    Be a dark, cool water calling—calling
To the footsore, benighted, solitary,
    When the shadows are falling.

O, be beauty for all my blindness,
    A moon in the air where the weary wend,
And dews burdened with loving-kindness
    In the dark of the end.

SOTTO VOCE

TO EDWARD THOMAS

The haze of noon wanned silver-grey
The soundless mansion of the sun:
The air made visible in his ray,
Like molten glass from furnace run,
Quivered o'er heat-baked turf and stone
And the flower of the gorse burned on—
Burned softly as gold of a child's fair hair
Along each spiky spray, and shed
Almond-like incense in the air
Whereon our senses fed.

At foot—a few sparse harebells: blue
And still as were the friend's dark eyes
That dwelt on mine, transfixèd through
With sudden ecstatic surmise.

'Hst!' he cried softly, smiling; and lo,
Stealing amidst that maze gold-green,
I heard a whispering music flow
From guileful throat of bird, unseen:—
So delicate the straining ear
Scarce carried its faint syllabling
Into a heart caught up to hear
That inmost pondering
Of bird-like self with self. We stood,
In happy trance-like solitude,
Hearkening a lullay grieved and sweet—
As when on isle uncharted beat
'Gainst coral at the palm-tree's root,
With brine-clear, snow-white foam afloat,

The wailing, not of water or wind—
A husht, far, wild, divine lament,
When Prospero his wizardry bent
Winged Ariel to bind. . . .

Then silence, and o'er-flooding noon.
I raised my head; smiled too. And he—
Moved his great hand, the magic gone—
Gently amused to see
My ignorant wonderment. He sighed.
'It was a nightingale,' he said,
'That *sotto voce* cons the song
He'll sing when dark is spread;
And Night's vague hours are sweet and long,
And we are laid abed.'

UNREGARDING

Put by thy days like withered flowers
    In twilight hidden away:
Memory shall up-build thee bowers
    Sweeter than they.

Hoard not from swiftness of thy stream
    The shallowest cruse of tears:
Pools still as heaven shall lovelier dream
    In future years.

FARE WELL

When I lie where shades of darkness
Shall no more assail mine eyes,
Nor the rain make lamentation
    When the wind sighs:
How will fare the world whose wonder
Was the very proof of me?
Memory fades, must the remembered
    Perishing be?

Oh, when this my dust surrenders
Hand, foot, lip, to dust again,
May these loved and loving faces
    Please other men!
May the rusting harvest hedgerow
Still the Traveller's Joy entwine,
And as happy children gather
    Posies once mine.

Look thy last on all things lovely,
Every hour. Let no night
Seal thy sense in deathly slumber
    Till to delight
Thou have paid thy utmost blessing;
Since that all things thou wouldst praise
Beauty took from those who loved them
    In other days.

MOTLEY

Come, Death, I'd have a word with thee;
And thou, poor Innocency;
And Love—a lad with broken wing;
And Pity, too:
The Fool shall sing to you,
As Fools will sing.

Ay, music hath small sense,
And a tune's soon told,
And Earth is old,
And my poor wits are dense;
Yet have I secrets,—dark, my dear,
To breathe you all. Come near.
And lest some hideous listener tells,
I'll ring my bells.

They are all at war!—
Yes, yes, their bodies go
'Neath burning sun and icy star
To chaunted songs of woe,
Dragging cold cannon through a mire
Of rain and blood and spouting fire,
The new moon glinting hard on eyes
Wide with insanities!

Ssh! . . . I use words
I hardly know the meaning of;
And the mute birds
Are glancing at Love
From out their shade of leaf and flower,
Trembling at treacheries
Which even in noonday cower.
Heed, heed not what I said

Of frenzied hosts of men,
More fools than I,
On envy, hatred fed,
Who kill, and die—
Spake I not plainly, then?
Yet Pity whispered, 'Why?'

Thou silly thing, off to thy daisies go!
Mine was not news for child to know,
And Death—no ears hath. He hath supped where creep
Eyeless worms in hush of sleep;
Yet, when he smiles, the hand he draws
Athwart his grinning jaws—
Faintly the thin bones rattle, and—there, there!
Hearken how my bells in the air
Drive away care! . . .

Nay, but a dream I had
Of a world all mad.
Not simple happy mad like me,
Who am mad like an empty scene
Of water and willow tree,
Where the wind hath been;
But that foul Satan-mad,
Who rots in his own head,
And counts the dead,
Not honest one—and two—
But for the ghosts they were,
Brave, faithful, true,
When, head in air,
In Earth's clear green and blue
Heaven they did share
With beauty who bade them there. . . .

There, now! Death goes—
Mayhap I've wearied him.
Ay, and the light doth dim;
And asleep's the rose;
And tired Innocence
In dreams is hence. . . .
Come, Love, my lad,
Nodding that drowsy head,
'Tis time thy prayers were said!

PEACE

Night is o'er England, and the winds are still;
Jasmine and honeysuckle steep the air;
Softly the stars that are all Europe's fill
Her heaven-wide dark with radiancy fair;
That shadowed moon now waxing in the west
Stirs not a rumour in her tranquil seas;
Mysterious sleep has lulled her heart to rest,
Deep even as theirs beneath her churchyard trees.

Secure, serene; dumb now the night-hawk's threat;
The guns' low thunder drumming o'er the tide;
The anguish pulsing in her stricken side. . . .
All is at peace. . . . But, never, heart, forget:
For this her youngest, best, and bravest died,
These bright dews once were mixed with bloody
    sweat.

BEFORE DAWN

Dim-berried is the mistletoe
With globes of sheenless grey,
The holly mid ten thousand thorns
Smoulders its fires away;
And in the manger Jesu sleeps
    This Christmas Day.

Bull unto bull with hollow throat
Makes echo every hill,
Cold sheep in pastures thick with snow
The air with bleatings fill;
While of his mother's heart this Babe
    Takes His sweet will.

All flowers and butterflies lie hid,
The blackbird and the thrush
Pipe but a little as they flit
Restless from bush to bush;
Even to the robin Gabriel hath
    Cried softly, 'Hush!'

Now night's astir with burning stars
In darkness of the snow;
Burdened with frankincense and myrrh
And gold the Strangers go
Into a dusk where one dim lamp
      Burns faintly, Lo!

No snowdrop yet its small head nods
In winds of winter drear;
No lark at casement in the sky
Sings matins shrill and clear;
Yet in this frozen mirk the Dawn
      Breathes, Spring is here!

GOOD-BYE

The last of last words spoken is, Good-bye—
The last dismantled flower in the weed-grown hedge,
The last thin rumour of a feeble bell far ringing,
The last blind rat to spurn the mildewed rye.

A hardening darkness glasses the haunted eye,
Shines into nothing the watcher's burnt-out candle,
Wreathes into scentless nothing the wasting incense,
Faints in the outer silence the hunting-cry.

Love of its muted music breathes no sigh,
Thought in her ivory tower gropes in her spinning,
Toss on in vain the whispering trees of Eden,
Last of all last words spoken is, Good-bye.

THE IMAGINATION'S PRIDE

Be not too wildly amorous of the far,
  Nor lure thy fantasy to its utmost scope.
Read by a taper when the needling star
  Burns red with menace in heaven's midnight cope.
Friendly thy body: guard its solitude.
  Sure shelter is thy heart. It once had rest
Where founts miraculous thy lips endewed,
  Yet nought loomed further than thy mother's breast.

O brave adventure! Ay, at danger slake
  Thy thirst, lest life in thee should, sickening, quail;
But not toward nightmare goad a mind awake,
  Nor to forbidden horizons bend thy sail—
Seductive outskirts whence in trance prolonged
  Thy gaze, at stretch of what is sane-secure,
Dreams out on steeps by shapes demoniac thronged
  And vales wherein alone the dead endure.

Nectarous those flowers, yet with venom sweet.
  Thick-juiced with poison hang those fruits that shine
Where sick phantasmal moonbeams brood and beat,
  And dark imaginations ripe the vine.
Bethink thee: every enticing league thou wend
  Beyond the mark where life its bound hath set
Will lead thee at length where human pathways end
  And the dark enemy spreads his maddening net.

Comfort thee, comfort thee. Thy Father knows
  How wild man's ardent spirit, fainting, yearns
For mortal glimpse of death's immortal rose,
  The garden where the invisible blossom burns.

Humble thy trembling knees; confess thy pride;
  Be weary. Oh, whithersoever thy vaunting rove,
His deepest wisdom harbours in thy side,
  In thine own bosom hides His utmost love.

THE VEIL

I think and think; yet still I fail—
Why does this lady wear a veil?
Why thus elect to mask her face
Beneath that dainty web of lace?
The tip of a small nose I see,
And two red lips, set curiously
Like twin-born cherries on one stem,
And yet she has netted even them.
Her eyes, it's plain, survey with ease
All that to glance upon they please.
Yet, whether hazel, grey, or blue,
Or that even lovelier lilac hue,
I cannot guess: why—why deny
Such beauty to the passer-by?
Out of a bush a nightingale
May expound his song; beneath that veil
A happy mouth no doubt can make
English sound sweeter for its sake.
But then, why muffle in, like this,
What every blossomy wind would kiss?
Why in that little night disguise
A daylight face, those starry eyes?

DRUGGED

Inert in his chair,
In a candle's guttering glow;
His bottle empty,
His fire sunk low;
With drug-sealed lids shut fast,
Unsated mouth ajar,
This darkened phantasm walks
Where nightmares are:

In a frenzy of life and light,
Criss-cross—a menacing throng—
They gibe, they squeal at the stranger.
Jostling along,
Their faces cadaverous grey:
While on high from an attic stare
Horrors, in beauty apparelled,
Down the dark air.

A stream gurgles over its stones,
The chambers within are a-fire.
Stumble his shadowy feet
Through shine, through mire;
And the flames leap higher.
In vain yelps the wainscot mouse;
In vain beats the hour;
Vacant, his body must drowse
Until daybreak flower—

Staining these walls with its rose,
And the draughts of the morning shall stir
Cold on cold brow, cold hands.
And the wanderer
Back to flesh house must return;
Lone soul—in horror to see,
Than dream more meagre and awful,
Reality.

THE VOICE

'We are not often alone, we two,'
Mused a secret voice in my ear,
As the dying hues of afternoon
Lapsed into evening drear.

A withered leaf, wafted on in the street,
Like a wayless spectre, sighed;
Aslant on the roof-tops a sickly moon
Did mutely abide.

Yet waste though the shallowing day might seem,
And fainter than hope its rose,
Strangely that speech in my thoughts welled on;
As water in-flows:

Like remembered words once heard in a room
Wherein death kept far-away tryst;
'Not often alone, we two; but thou,
How sorely missed!'

QUIET

Mutely the mole toils on;
The worm in silk cocoon
Stealthy as spider spins,
    As glides the moon.
But listen where envy peers 'neath the half-closed lid;
Where peeping vanity lurks; where pride lies hid;
And peace beyond telling share with the light-stilled eye,
When naught but an image of the loved one's nigh.

THE FLOWER

Horizon to horizon, lies outspread
The tenting firmament of day and night;
Wherein are winds at play; and planets shed
Amid the stars their gentle gliding light.

The huge world's sun flames on the snow-capped hills;
Cindrous his heat burns in the sandy plain;
With myriad spume-bows roaring ocean swills
The cold profuse abundance of the rain.

And man—a transient object in this vast,
Sighs o'er a universe transcending thought,
Afflicted by vague bodings of the past,
Driven toward a future, unforeseen, unsought.

Yet, see him, stooping low to naked weed
That meeks its blossom in his anxious eye,
Mark how he grieves, as if his heart did bleed,
And wheels his wondrous features to the sky;
As if, transfigured by so small a grace,
He sought Companion in earth's dwelling-place.

AN EPITAPH

Last, Stone, a little yet;
And then this dust forget.
But thou, fair Rose, bloom on.
For she who is gone
Was lovely too; nor would she grieve to be
Sharing in solitude her dreams with thee.

THE QUIET ENEMY

Hearken!—now the hermit bee
Drones a quiet threnody;
Greening on the stagnant pool
The criss-cross light slants silken-cool;
In the venomed yew tree wings
Preen and flit. The linnet sings.

Gradually the brave sun
Droops to a day's journey done;
In the marshy flats abide
Mists to muffle midnight-tide.
Puffed within the belfry tower
Hungry owls drowse out their hour. . . .

Walk in beauty. Vaunt thy rose.
Flaunt thy transient loveliness.
Pace for pace with thee there goes
A shape that hath not come to bless.
I thine enemy? . . . Nay, nay.
I can only watch and wait
Patient treacherous time away,
Hold ajar the wicket gate.

THE LAST COACHLOAD

TO COLIN

Crashed through the woods that lumbering Coach. The dust
Of flinted roads bepowdering felloe and hood.
Its gay paint cracked, its axles red with rust,
It lunged, lurched, toppled through a solitude

Of whispering boughs, and feathery, nid-nod grass.
Plodded the fetlocked horses. Glum and mum,
Its ancient Coachman recked not where he was,
Nor into what strange haunt his wheels were come.

Crumbling the leather of his dangling reins;
Worn to a cow's tuft his stumped, idle whip;
Sharp eyes of beast and bird in the trees' green lanes
Gleamed out like stars above a derelict ship.

'Old Father Time—Time—Time!' jeered twittering throat.
A squirrel capered on the leader's rump,
Slithered a weasel, peered a thief-like stoat,
In sandy warren beat on the coney's thump.

Mute as a mammet in his saddle sate
The hunched Postilion, clad in magpie trim;
The bright flies buzzed around his hairless pate;
Yaffle and jay squawked mockery at him.

Yet marvellous peace and amity breathed there.
Tranquil the labyrinths of this sundown wood.
Musking its chaces, bloomed the brier-rose fair;
Spellbound as if in trance the pine-trees stood.

Through moss and pebbled rut the wheels rasped on;
That Ancient drowsing on his box. And still
The bracken track with glazing sunbeams shone;
Laboured the horses, straining at the hill. . . .

But now—a verdurous height with eve-shade sweet;
Far, far to West the Delectable Mountains glowed.
Above, Night's canopy; at the horses' feet
A sea-like honied waste of flowers flowed.

There fell a pause of utter quiet. And—
Out from one murky window glanced an eye,
Stole from the other a lean, groping hand,
The padded door swung open with a sigh. ·

And—*Exeunt Omnes!* None to ask the fare—
A myriad human Odds in a last release
Leap out incontinent, snuff the incensed air;
A myriad parched-up voices whisper, 'Peace'.

On, on, and on—a stream, a flood, they flow.
O wondrous vale of jocund buds and bells!
Like vanishing smoke the rainbow legions glow,
Yet still the enravished concourse sweeps and swells.

All journeying done. Rest now from lash and spur—
Laughing and weeping, shoulder and elbow—'twould seem
That Coach capacious all Infinity were,
And these the fabulous figments of a dream.

Mad for escape; frenzied each breathless mote,
Lest rouse the Old Enemy from his death-still swoon,
Lest crack that whip again—they fly, they float,
Scamper, breathe—'Paradise!' abscond, are gone. . . .

FOREBODING

Thou canst not see him standing by—
    Time—with a poppied hand
Stealing thy youth's simplicity,
Even as falls unceasingly
    His waning sand.

He'll pluck thy childish roses, as
    Summer from her bush
Strips all the loveliness that was;
Even to the silence evening has
    Thy laughter hush.

Thy locks too faint for earthly gold,
    The meekness of thine eyes,
He will darken and dim, and to his fold
Drive, 'gainst the night, thy stainless, old
    Innocencies;

Thy simple words confuse and mar,
    Thy tenderest thoughts delude
Draw a long cloud athwart thy star,
Still with loud timbrels heaven's far
    Faint interlude.

Thou canst not see; I see, dearest;
    O, then, yet patient be,
Though love refuse thy heart all rest,
Though even love work angry, lest
    Love should lose *thee*!

I SIT ALONE

I sit alone,
And clear thoughts move in me,
Pictures, now near, now far,
Of transient fantasy.
Happy I am, at peace
In my own company.

Yet life is a dread thing, too,
Dark with horror and fear.
Beauty's fingers grow cold,
Sad cries I hear,
Death with a stony gaze
Is ever near.

Lost in myself I hide
From the cold unknown:
Lost, like a world cast forth
Into space star-sown:
And the songs of the morning are stilled,
And delight in them flown.

So even the tender and dear
Like phantoms through memory stray—
Creations of sweet desire,
That faith can alone bid stay:
They cast off the cloak of the real
And vanish away.

Only love can redeem
This truth, that delight;
Bring morning to blossom again
Out of plague-ridden night;
Restore to the lost the found,
To the blinded, sight.

THE RAILWAY JUNCTION

From here through tunnelled gloom the track
Forks into two; and one of these
Wheels onward into darkening hills,
And one toward distant seas.

How still it is; the signal light
At set of sun shines palely green;
A thrush sings; other sound there's none,
Nor traveller to be seen—

Where late there was a throng. And now,
In peace awhile, I sit alone;
Though soon, at the appointed hour,
I shall myself be gone.

But not their way: the bow-legged groom,
The parson in black, the widow and son,

The sailor with his cage, the gaunt
Gamekeeper with his gun,

That fair one, too, discreetly veiled—
All, who so mutely came, and went,
Will reach those far nocturnal hills,
Or shores, ere night is spent.

I nothing know why thus we met—
Their thoughts, their longings, hopes, their fate:
And what shall I remember, except—
The evening growing late—

That here through tunnelled gloom the track
Forks into two; of these
One into darkening hills leads on,
And one toward distant seas?

'HOW SLEEP THE BRAVE'

Bitterly, England must thou grieve—
  Though none of these poor men who died
But did within his soul believe
  That death for thee was glorified.

Ever they watched it hovering near—
  A mystery beyond thought to plumb—
And often, in loathing and in fear,
  They heard cold danger whisper, Come!—

Heard, and obeyed. Oh, if thou weep
  Such courage and honour, woe, despair;
Remember too that those who sleep
  No more remorse can share.

A YOUNG GIRL

I search in vain your childlike face to see
The thoughts that hide behind the words you say;
I hear them singing, but close-shut from me
Dream the enchanted woods through which they stray.
Cheek, lip, and brow—I glance from each to each,
And watch that light-winged Mercury, your hand;
And sometimes when brief silence falls on speech
I seem your hidden self to understand.

Mine a dark fate. Behind his iron bars
The captive broods, with ear and heart a-strain
For jangle of key, for glimpse of moon or stars,
Grey shaft of daylight, sighing of the rain.
Life built these walls. Past all my dull surmise
Must burn the inward innocence of your eyes.

THE ENCOUNTER

'Twixt dream and wake we wandered on,
Thinking of naught but you and me;
And lo, when day was nearly gone,
 A wondrous sight did see.

There, in a bed of rushes, lay
A child all naked, golden and fair—
Young Eros dreaming time away,
 With roses in his hair.

Tender sleep had o'ertaken him,
Quenched his bright arrows, loosed his bow,
And in divine oblivion dim
 Had stilled him through and through.

Never have I such beauty seen
As burned in his young dreaming face,

Cheek, hair, and lip laid drowsily
    In slumber's faint embrace.

Oh, how he started, how his eyes
Caught back their sudden shiningness
To see you stooping, loving-wise,
    Him, slumbering, to caress!

How flamed his brow, what childish joy
Leapt in his heart at sight of thee
When, 'Mother, Mother!' cried the boy:
    And—frowning—turned on me!

ROSE

Three centuries now are gone
    Since Thomas Campion
Left men his airs, his verse, his heedful prose.
    Few other memories
    Have we of him, or his,
And, of his sister, none, but that her name was Rose.

Woodruff, far moschatel
    May the more fragrant smell
When into brittle dust their blossoming goes.
    His, too, a garden sweet,
    Where rarest beauties meet,
And, as a child, he shared them with this Rose.

Faded, past changing, now,
    Cheek, mouth, and childish brow.
Where, too, her phantom wanders no man knows.
    Yet, when in undertone
    That eager lute pines on,
Pleading of things he loved, it sings of Rose.

73

THE STRANGE SPIRIT

Age shall not daunt me, nor sorrow for youth that is gone
If thou lead on before me;
If thy voice in the darkness and bleak of that final night
Still its enchantment weave o'er me.
Thou hauntest the stealing shadow of rock and tree;
Hovering on wings invisible smilest at me;
Fannest the secret scent of the moth-hung flower;
Making of musky eve thy slumber-bower.

But not without danger thy fleeting presence abides
In a mind lulled in dreaming.
Lightning bepictures thy gaze. When the thunder raves,
And the tempest rain is streaming,
Betwixt cloud and earth thy falcon-head leans near—
Menacing earth-bound spirit betrayed to fear.
Cold then as shadow of death, that icy glare
Pierces the window of sense to the chamber bare.

Busied o'er dust, engrossed o'er the clod-close root,
Fire of the beast in conflict bleeding,
Goal of the coursing fish on its ocean tryst,
Wind of the weed's far seeding,
Whose servant art thou? Who gave thee earth, sky and sea
For uttermost kingdom and ranging? Who bade thee to be
Bodiless, lovely; snare, and delight of the soul,
Fantasy's beacon, of thought the uttermost goal?

When I told my love thou wert near, she bowed, and sighed.
With passion her pale face darkened.
Trembling the lips that to mine in silence replied;
Sadly that music she hearkened.

Miracle thine the babe in her bosom at rest,
Flowerlike, hidden loose-folded on gentle breast—
And we laughed together in quiet, unmoved by fear,
Knowing that, life of life, thou wast hovering near.

SNOWING

Snowing; snowing;
Oh, between earth and sky
A wintry wind is blowing,
Scattering with its sigh
Petals from trees of silver that shine
Like invisible glass, when the moon
In the void of night on high
Paces her orchards divine.

Snowing; snowing;
Ah me, how still, and how fair
The air with flakes interflowing,
The fields crystal and bare,
When the brawling brooks are dumb
And the parched trees matted with frost,
And the birds in this wilderness stare
    Dazzled and numb!

Snowing . . . snowing . . . snowing:
Moments of time through space
Into hours, centuries growing,
Till the world's marred lovely face,
Wearied of change and chance,
Radiant in innocence dream—
Lulled by an infinite grace
To rest in eternal trance.

THE SNOWDROP

Now—now, as low I stooped, thought I,
I will see what this snowdrop *is;*
So shall I put much argument by,
      And solve a lifetime's mysteries.

A northern wind had frozen the grass;
Its blades were hoar with crystal rime,
Aglint like light-dissecting glass
      At beam of morning-prime.

From hidden bulb the flower reared up
Its angled, slender, cold, dark stem,
Whence dangled an inverted cup
      For tri-leaved diadem.

Beneath these ice-pure sepals lay
A triplet of green-pencilled snow,
Which in the chill-aired gloom of day
      Stirred softly to and fro.

Mind fixed, but else made vacant, I,
Lost to my body, called my soul
To don that frail solemnity,
      Its inmost self my goal.

And though in vain—no mortal mind
Across that threshold yet hath fared!—
In this collusion I divined
      Some consciousness we shared.

Strange roads—while suns, a myriad, set—
Had led us through infinity;
And where they crossed, there then had met
    Not two of us, but three.

THE FLEETING

The late wind failed; high on the hill
The pine's resounding boughs were still:
Those wondrous airs that space had lent
To wail earth's night-long banishment
From heat and light and song of day
In a last sighing died away.

Alone in the muteness, lost and small,
I watched from far-off Leo fall
An ebbing trail of silvery dust,
And fade to naught; while, near and far,
Glittered in quiet star to star;
And dreamed, in midnight's dim immense,
Heaven's universal innocence.

O transient heart that yet can raise
To the unseen its pang of praise,
And from the founts in play above
Be freshed with that sweet love!

THE ROUND

I watched, upon a vase's rim,
An earwig—strayed from honeyed cell—
Circling a track once strange to him,
    But now known far too well.

With vexed antennae, searching space,
And giddy grope to left and right,
On—and still on—he pressed apace,
    Out of, and into, sight.

In circumambulation drear,
He neither wavered, paused nor stayed;
But now kind Providence drew near—
    A slip of wood I laid

Across his track. He scaled its edge:
And soon was safely restored to where
A sappy, dew-bright, flowering hedge
    Of dahlias greened the air.

Ay, and as apt may be my fate! . . .
Smiling, I turned to work again:
But shivered, where in shade I sate,
    And idle did remain.

WHAT?

What dost thou surely know?
What will the truth remain,
When from the world of men thou go
To the unknown again?

What science—of what hope?
What heart-loved certitude won
From thought shall then for scope
Be thine—thy thinking done?

'Tis said, that even the wise
When plucking at the sheet,
Have smiled with swift-darkening eyes,
As if in vision fleet

Of some mere flower, or bird,
Seen in dream, or in childhood's play;
And then, without sign or word,
Have turned from the world away.

TO K.M.

And there was a horse in the king's stables: and the name of the horse was, Genius.

We sat and talked. . . It was June, and the summer light
Lay fair upon ceiling and wall as the day took flight.
Tranquil the room—with its colours and shadows wan,
Cherries, and china, and flowers: and the hour slid on.
Dark hair, dark eyes, slim fingers—you made the tea,
Pausing with spoon uplifted, to speak to me.
Lulled by our thoughts and our voices, how happy were we!

And, musing, an old, old riddle crept into my head.
'Supposing I just say, *Horse in a field*,' I said,
'What do you *see*?' And we each made answer: 'I—
A roan—long tail, and a red-brick house, near by.'
'I—an old cart-horse and rain!' 'Oh no, not rain;
A mare with a long-legged foal by a pond—oh plain!'
'And I, a hedge—and an elm—and the shadowy green
Sloping gently up to the blue, to the west, I mean!' . . .

And now: on the field that I see, night's darkness lies.
A brook brawls near: there are stars in the empty skies.
The grass is deep, and dense. As I push my way,
From sour-nettled ditch sweeps fragrance of clustering may.
I come to a stile. And lo, on the further side,
With still, umbrageous, night-clad fronds, spread wide,
A giant cedar broods. And in crescent's gleam—
A horse, milk-pale, sleek-shouldered, engendered of dream!
Startled, it lifts its muzzle, deep eyes agaze,
Silk-plaited mane . . .

                    'Whose pastures are thine to graze?
Creature, delicate, lovely, with woman-like head,
Sphinx-like, gazelle-like? Where tarries thy rider?' I said.

And I scanned by that sinking slip's thin twinkling shed
A high-pooped saddle of leather, night-darkened red,
Stamped with a pattern of gilding; and over it thrown
A cloak, chain-buckled, with one great glamorous stone,
Wan as the argent moon when o'er fields of wheat
Like Dian she broods, and steals to Endymion's feet.
Interwoven with silver that cloak from seam to seam.
And at toss of that head from its damascened bridle did beam
Mysterious glare in the dead of the dark. . . .
              'Thy name,
Fantastical steed? Thy pedigree?
Peace, out of Storm, is the tale? Or *Beauty, of Jeopardy?*'

The water grieves. Not a footfall—and midnight here.
Why tarries Darkness's bird? Mounded and clear
Slopes to yon hill with its stars the moorland sweet.
There sigh the airs of far heaven. And the dreamer's feet
Scatter the leagues of paths secret to where at last meet
Roads called Wickedness, Righteousness, broad-flung or strait,
And the third that leads on to the Queen of fair Elfland's gate. . . .

This then the horse that I see; swift as the wind;
That none may master or mount; and none may bind—
But she, his Mistress: cloaked, and at throat that gem—
Dark hair, dark eyes, slim shoulder. . . .
              God-speed, K. M.!

THE VISIONARY

There is a pool whose waters clear
Reflect not what is standing near;
The silver-banded birch, the grass
Find not therein a looking-glass;
Nor doth Orion, pacing night,
Scatter thereon his wintry light.
Nor ever to its darnelled brink
Comes down the hare or deer to drink;
Sombre and secret it doth keep
Stilled in unshaken, crystal sleep.

But once, a Wanderer, parched, forlorn,
Worn with night-wayfaring, came at morn,
By pathless thickets grey with dew;
And stooping at its margent blue
To lave his wearied eyes, discerned
Somewhat that in the water burned—
A face like amber, pale and still,
With eyes of light, unchangeable,
Whose grave and steadfast scrutiny
Pierced through all earthly memory.

Voiceless and windless the green wood,
Above its shadowy quietude,
Sighed faintly through its unfading leaves;
And still he stooped; and still he yearned
To kiss the lips that therein burned;
To close those eyes that from the deep
Gazed on him, wearied out for sleep.

He drank; he slumbered; and he went
Back into life's wild banishment,
Like one whose every thought may seem
The wreckage of a wasting dream;

All savour gone from life, delight
Charged with foreboding dark as night;
Love but the memory of what
Woke once, but reawakens not.

THE SPARK

Calm was the evening, as if asleep,
But sickled on high with brooding storm,
Couched in invisible space. And, lo!
I saw in utter silence sweep
Out of that darkening starless vault
A gliding spark, as blanched as snow,
That burned into dust, and vanished in
A hay-cropped meadow, brightly green.

A meteor from the cold of space,
Lost in Earth's wilderness of air?—
Presage of lightnings soon to shine
In splendour on this lonely place?—
I cannot tell; but only how fair
It glowed within the crystalline
Pure heavens, and of its strangeness lit
My mind to joy at sight of it.

Yet, what is common, as lovely may be:
The petalled daisy, a honey bell,
A pebble, a branch of moss, a gem
Of mist, or fallen rain—if we
A moment in their beauty dwell;
Entranced, alone, see only them. . . .
How blind to wait, till, merely unique,
Some omen thus the all bespeak!

A BALLAD OF CHRISTMAS

It was about the deep of night,
  And still was earth and sky,
When in the moonlight, dazzling bright,
  Three ghosts came riding by.

Beyond the sea—beyond the sea,
  Lie kingdoms for them all:
I wot their steeds trod wearily—
  The journey is not small.

By rock and desert, strand and stream,
  They footsore late did go:
Now, like a sweet and blessed dream,
  Their path was deep with snow.

Shining like hoarfrost, rode they on,
  Three ghosts in earth's array:
It was about the hour when wan
  Night turns at hint of day.

Oh, but their hearts with woe distraught
  Hailed not the wane of night,
Only for Jesu still they sought
  To wash them clean and white.

For bloody was each hand, and dark
  With death each orbless eye;—
It was three Traitors mute and stark
  Came riding silent by.

Silver their raiment and their spurs,
  And silver-shod their feet,
And silver-pale each face that stared
  Into the moonlight sweet.

And he upon the left that rode
   Was Pilate, Prince of Rome,
Whose journey once lay far abroad,
   And now was nearing home.

And he upon the right that rode,
   Herod of Salem sate,
Whose mantle dipped in children's blood
   Shone clear as Heaven's gate.

And he, these twain betwixt, that rode
   Was clad as white as wool,
Dyed in the Mercy of his God,
   White was he crown to sole.

Throned mid a myriad Saints in bliss
   Rise shall the Babe of Heaven
To shine on these three ghosts, i-wis,
   Smit through with sorrows seven;

Babe of the Blessed Trinity
   Shall smile their steeds to see:
Herod and Pilate riding by,
   And Judas, one of three.

MEMORY

When summer heat has drowsed the day
With blaze of noontide overhead,
And hidden greenfinch can but say
What but a moment since it said;
When harvest fields stand thick with wheat,
And wasp and bee slave—dawn till dark—
Nor home, till evening moonbeams beat,
Silvering the nightjar's oaken bark:
How strangely then the mind may build
A magic world of wintry cold,
Its meadows with frail frost-flowers filled—
Bright-ribbed with ice, a frozen wold! . . .

When dusk shuts in the shortest day,
And huge Orion spans the night;
Where antlered fireflames leap and play
Chequering the walls with fitful light—
Even sweeter in mind the summer's rose
May bloom again; her drifting swan
Resume her beauty; while rapture flows
Of birds long since to silence gone:
And though the Nowel, sharp and shrill,
Of Waits from out the snowbound street,
Drums to their fiddle beneath the hill
June's mill-wheel where the waters meet . . .

O angel Memory that can
Double the joys of faithless Man!

Spake the fire-tinged bramble, bossed with gleaming fruit and
   blossoming,
   Gently serpentining in the air a blunted tongue:—
'Far too long these bones I hide have blackened in my covert
   here,
   Too long their noxious odour to my sweetness now hath
   clung.
Would they were gross clay, and their evil spell removed
   from me;
   How much lovelier I, if my roots not thence had sprung.'

Breathed the wind of sundown, 'Ay, this haunt is long years
   sour to me;
   But naught on earth that's human can my fancy free
   beguile.
Wings are mine far fleeter than the birds' that clip these
   branches;
   Arabian rich the burden which for honeyed mile on mile
Is wafted on my bosom, hill to ocean, wood to valeland.
   Anathema on relics that my fragrances defile!'

Stirred a thousand frondlets and the willow tree replied to it:—
   'Sty and mixen, foetid pool, and carrion-shed—whose these?
Yet earth makes sweet the foulest; naught—naught stays long
   unclean to her;
   Thou, too, howe'er reluctant, art her servant, gliding Breeze.
Restrain thy fretting pudency; in pity sigh for one I knew—
   The woman whose unburied bones in thornbrake take their
   ease.'

'*Urkkh*: when dark hath thicked to night,' croaked vermin toad that crouched near-by,
  'And the stars that mock in heaven unto midnight's cope have clomb,
When the shades of all the humans that in life were brutal foes to me
  Lift thready lamentation from the churchyard's rancid loam—
Return doth she in mortal guise 'gainst whom I bear no enmity
  Foredoomed by fate this treacherous field for aye to haunt and roam.'

'Pictured once her image I,' sang sliding brook its rushes from,
  'That sallow face, and eyes that seemed to stare as if in dream,
Narrow shoulders, long lean hands, and hair like withered grass in hue,
  Pale lips drawn thwart with grieving in stars' silver mocking beam.
Once, too, I heard her story, but little I remember now,
  Though the blood that gave her power to suffer then imbrued my stream.'

Stony rock groaned forth its voice, 'No mirror featly shattered I,
  Blind I am by nature, but, I boast, not deaf or dumb;
Small truck I pay to Time's decay, nor mark what wounds black winter makes.
  Not mine to know what depths of snow have thawed and left me numb—
Since an eve when flowers had cast their seed, and evening cooled my brow again,
  And I echoed to a voice that whispered, "Loved one, I have come." '

Wafting through the woodland swept an owl from out the
  silentness,
  '*Too wittoo woo*,' she hooted. 'A human comes this way,
Gliding as on feathered heel, so tenuous that the thorns she
    skirts
    To eyes bright-glassed for glooms like mine show black be-
      yond her grey.
A tryst she keeps. Beware, good friends, not mine day's mortal
    company,
    Hungry my brood for juicier fare,' she squawked, and
    plumed away.

Lone, in a shoal of milk-white cloud, bathed now the punctual
    fickle moon
    That nook of brook and willow, long unpolled, with silvery
      glare:—
'Unstilled yet tranquil Phantom, see, thou canst not hide thy
    form from me:
    When last thy anguished body trod these meadows fresh
    and fair,
I, the ringing sand-dunes of the vast Sahara hoared with light:
    What secret calls thee from the shades; why hither dost
      thou fare?' . . .

Small beauty graced the spectre pondering mute beneath the
    willow-boughs
    O'er relics long grown noisome to the bramble and the
    breeze;
A hand upon her narrow breast, her head bent low in shadow-
    iness;
    'I've come,' sighed voice like muted bell of nightbird in the
    trees,
'To tell again for all to hear, the wild remorse that suffers me,
    No single thought of rest or hope whereon to muse at ease.

'Self-slaughtered I, for one I loved, who could not give me
love again,
   Uncounted now the Autumns since that twilight hour
   malign
When, insensate for escape from a hunger naught could satisfy,
   I vowed to God no more would I in torment live and pine.
Alas! He turned His face away, and woeful penance laid on
me—
   That every night make tryst must I till life my love resign.'

Furtive fell the anxious glance she cast that dreadful hiding-
place;
   Strangely still and muted ceased the tones in which she spake.
Shadow filled her vacant place. The moon withdrew in cloud
again.
   Hushed the ripples grieving to the pebbles in their wake.
'Thus her *tale*!' quoth sod to sod. 'Not ours, good friends, to
challenge it;
   Though her blood still cries for vengeance on her murderer
   from this brake!'

THE OWL

'Well, God 'ild you! They say the owle was a baker's daughter.'
Hamlet, IV, v.

The door-bell jangled in evening's peace,
Its clapper dulled with verdigris.
Lit by the hanging lamp's still flame
Into the shop a beggar came,
Glanced gravely around him—counter, stool,
Ticking clock and heaped-up tray
Of baker's dainties, put to cool;
And quietly turned his eyes away.

Stepped out the goodwife from within—
Her blandest smile from brow to chin
Fading at once to blank chagrin
As she paused to peer, with keen blue eyes
Sharpened to find a stranger there,
And one, she knew, no customer.
'We never give . . .' she said, and stayed;
Mute and intent, as if dismayed
At so profoundly still a face.
'What do you want?' She came a pace
Nearer, and scanned him, head to foot.
He looked at her, but answered not.

The tabby-cat that, fathom deep,
On the scoured counter lay asleep,
Reared up its head to yawn, and then,
Composing itself to sleep again,
With eyes by night made black as jet,
Gazed on the stranger. 'A crust,' he said.
    'A crust of bread.'
Disquiet in the woman stirred—
No plea, or plaint, or hinted threat—

So low his voice she had scarcely heard.
She shook her head; he turned to go.
'We've nothing here for beggars. And so . . .
If we gave food to all who come
They'd eat us out of house and home—
Where charity begins, they say;
And ends, as like as not—or may.'
Still listening, he answered not,
His eyes upon the speaker set,
Eyes that she tried in vain to evade
    But had not met.
She frowned. 'Well, that's my husband's rule;
But stay a moment. There's a stool—
Sit down and wait. Stale bread we've none.
And else . . .' she shrugged. 'Still, rest awhile,'
Her smooth face conjured up a smile,
'And I'll go see what can be done.'

He did as he was bidden. And she
Went briskly in, and shut the door;
To pause, in brief uncertainty,
Searching for what she failed to find.
Then tiptoed back to peer once more
In through the ribboned muslin blind,
And eyed him secretly, askance,
With a prolonged, keen, searching glance;
As if mere listening might divine
Some centuries-silent countersign . . .
Scores of lean hungry folk she had turned
Even hungrier from her door, though less
From stint and scorn than heedlessness.
Why then should she a scruple spare
For one who, in a like distress,
Had spoken as if in heart he yearned
Far more for peace than bread? But now

No mark of gloom obscured his brow,
No shadow of darkness or despair.
Still as an image of age-worn stone
That from a pinnacle looks down
Over the seas of time, he sat;
His stooping face illumined by
The burnished scales that hung awry
Beside the crusted loaves of bread.
Never it seemed shone lamp so still
  On one so sore bestead.
'Poor wretch,' she muttered, 'he minds me of . . .'
A footfall sounded from above;
And, hand on mouth, immovable,
She watched and pondered there until,
Stepping alertly down the stair,
Her daughter—young as she was fair—
Came within earshot.
                'H'st,' she cried.
'A stranger here! And Lord betide,
He may have been watching till we're alone,
Biding his time, your father gone.
Come, now; come quietly and peep!—
Rags!—he would make a Christian weep!
I've promised nothing; but, good lack!
What shall I say when I go back?'

Her daughter softly stepped to peep.
'Pah! begging,' she whispered; 'I know that tale.
Money is all he wants—for ale!'
Through the cold glass there stole a beam
Of lamplight on her standing there,
Stilling her beauty as in a dream.
It smote to gold her wing-soft hair,
It scarleted her bird-bright cheek,
With shadow tinged her childlike neck,

Dreamed on her rounded bosom, and lay—
Like a sapphire pool at break of day,
Where martin and wagtail preen and play—
In the shallow shining of her eye.

'T't, mother,' she scoffed, with a scornful sigh,
And peeped again, and sneered—her lip
Drawn back from her small even teeth,
Showing the bright-red gums beneath.
'Look, now! The wretch has fallen asleep—
Stark at the counter, there; still as death.
As I sat alone at my looking-glass,
I heard a footstep—watched him pass,
Turn, and limp thief-like back again.
Out went my candle. I listened; and then
Those two faint *dings*. Aha! thought I,
Honest he may be, though old and blind,
But *that's* no customer come to buy.
So down I came—too late! I knew
He'd get less comfort from me than you!
I warrant, a pretty tale he told!
"Alone"! Lord love us! Leave him to me.
I'll teach him manners. Wait and see.'
She nodded her small snake-like head,
Sleeked with its strands of palest gold,
'Waste not, want not, say I,' she said.
Her mother faltered. Their glances met—
Furtive and questioning; hard and cold—
In mute communion mind with mind,
Though little to share could either find.
'Save us!' she answered, 'sharp eyes you have,
If in the dark you can see the blind!
He was as tongueless as the grave.
"Tale"! Not a sigh. Not one word said.
  Except that he asked for bread.'

Uneasy in her thoughts, she yet
Knew, howsoever late the hour,
And none in call, small risk they ran
From any homeless beggar-man.
While as for this—worn, wasted, wan—
A nod, and he'd be gone.
Waste not, want not, forsooth! The chit—
To think that she should so dictate!

' "Asleep," you say? Well, what of that?
What mortal harm can come of it?
A look he gave me; and his eyes . . .
Leave him to me, Miss Worldly-wise!
Trouble him not. Stay here, while I
See how much broken meat's put by.
God knows the wretch may have his fill.
And you—keep watch upon the till!'

She hastened in, with muffled tread.
Meanwhile her daughter, left alone,
Waited, watching, till she was gone;
Then softly drew open the door, to stare
More nearly through the sombre air
At the still face, dark matted hair,
Scarred hand, shut eyes, and silent mouth,
Parched with the long day's bitter drouth;
Now aureoled in the lustre shed
From the murky lamp above his head.
Her tense young features distorted, she
Gazed on, in sharpening enmity,
Her eager lips tight shut, as if
The very air she breathed might be
Poisoned by this foul company.
That such should be allowed to live!
Yet, as she watched him, needle-clear,

Beneath her contempt stirred fear.
Fear, not of body's harm, or aught
Instinct or cunning may have taught
Wits edged by watchful vanity:
It seemed her inmost soul made cry—
Wild thing, bewildered, the huntsmen nigh—
Of hidden ambush, and a flood
Of vague forebodings chilled her blood.
Kestrel keen, her eyes' bright blue
Narrowed, as she stole softly through.

'H'st, you!' she whispered him. 'Waken! Hear!
I come to warn you. Danger's near!'
Cat-like she scanned him, drew-to the door,
'She is calling for help. No time to wait!—
Before the neighbours come—before
They hoick their dogs on, and it's too late!'
The stranger listened; turned; and smiled:
'But whither shall I go, my child?
All ways are treacherous to those
Who, seeking friends, find only foes.'

My child!—the words like poison ran
Through her quick mind. 'What!' she began,
In fuming rage; then stayed; for, lo,
This visage, for all its starven woe,
That now met calmly her scrutiny,
Of time's corruption was wholly free.
The eyes beneath the level brows,
Though weary for want of sleep, yet shone
With strange directness, gazing on.
In her brief life she had never seen
A face so eager yet serene,
And, in its deathless courage, none
To bear with it comparison.

'I will begone,' at length he said.
  'All that I asked was bread.'

Her anger died away; she sighed;
Pouted; then laughed. 'So Mother tried
To scare me? Told me I must stop
In there—some wretch was in the shop
Who'd come to rob and. . . . Well, thought I,
Seeing's believing; I could but try
To keep *her* safe. What else to do—
Till help might come?' She paused, and drew
A straying lock of yellow hair
Back from her cheek—as palely fair—
In heedless indolence; as when
A wood-dove idly spreads her wing
Sunwards, and folds it in again.
Aimless, with fingers slender and cold,
She fondled the tress more stealthily
  Than miser with his gold.
And still her wonder grew: to see
A man of this rare courtesy
So sunken in want and poverty.
What was his actual errand here?
And whereto was he journeying?
A silence had fallen between them. Save
The weight-clock's ticking, slow and grave,
No whisper, in or out, she heard;
The cat slept on; and nothing stirred.
'Is it only hungry?' she cajoled,
In this strange quiet made more bold.
'Far worse than hunger seems to me
The cankering fear of growing old.
That is a kind of hunger too—
Which even *I* can share with you.
And, heaven help me, always alone!

Mother cares nothing for that. But wait;
See now how dark it is, and late;
Nor any roof for shelter. But soon
Night will be lovely—with the moon.
When all is quiet, and she abed,
Do you come back, and click the latch;
And I'll sit up above, and watch.
A supper then I'll bring,' she said,
'Sweeter by far than mouldy bread!'

Like water chiming in a well
Which uncropped weeds more sombre make,
The low seductive syllables fell
        Of every word she spake—
Music lulling the listening ear,
Note as of nightbird, low and clear,
        That yet keeps grief awake.
But still he made no sign. And she,
Now fearing his silence, scoffed mockingly,
'God knows I'm not the one to give
For the mere asking. As I live
I loathe the cringing skulking scum,
Day in, day out, that begging come;
Sots, tramps, who pester, whine, and shirk—
They'd rather starve to death than work.
And lie!'—She aped, ' "God help me, m'm;
'Tisn't myself but them at home!
Crying for food they are. Yes, seven!—
And their poor mother safe in heaven!" '
Glib as a prating parrot she
Mimicked the words with sidling head,
Bright-red tongue and claw-like hands.
'But—I can tell you—when I'm there
There's little for the seven to share!'
She raised her eyebrows; innocent, mild—

Less parrot now than pensive child;
Her every movement of body and face,
As of a flower in the wind's embrace,
   Born of a natural grace.
A vagrant moth on soundless plume,
Lured by the quiet flame within,
Fanned darkling through the narrow room,
Out of the night's obscurity.
   She watched it vacantly.
'If we gave food to *all*, you see
We might as well a Workhouse be!
I've not much patience with beggary.
What use is it to whine and wail?—
Most things in this world are made for sale!
But one who really needs. . . .' She sighed.
'I'd hate for him to be denied.'
She smoothed her lips, then smiled, to say:
'Have you yourself come far to-day?'
Like questing call, where shallows are
And sea-birds throng, rang out that *far*—
Decoy to every wanderer.

The stranger turned, and looked at her.
'Far, my child; and far must fare.
My only home is everywhere;
   And that the homeless share:
The vile, the lost, in misery—
   Where comfort cannot be.
You are young, your life's your own to spend;
May it escape as dark an end.'

Her fickle heart fell cold, her eyes
Stirred not a hair's breadth, serpent-wise.
'You say', she bridled, 'that to me!
Meaning you'd have their company

Rather than mine? Why, when a friend
Gives for the giving, there's an end
To that dull talk! *My child!*—can't you
See who you are talking to?
Do you suppose because I stop
Caged up in this dull village shop
With none but clods and numskulls near,
Whose only thought is pig and beer,
And sour old maids that pry and leer,
I am content? Me! Never pine
For what by every right is mine?
Had I a wild-sick bird to keep,
Is this where she should mope and cheep?
Aching, starving, for love and light,
Eating her heart out, dawn to night!
Oh, yes, they say that safety's sweet;
And groundsel—something good to eat!
But, Lord! I'd outsing the morning stars,
For a lump of sugar between the bars!
I loathe this life. "*My child!*" *You* see!
Wait till she's dead—and I am free!'
Aghast, she stayed—her young cheeks blenched,
Mouth quivering, and fingers clenched—
'What right have you . . .?' she challenged, and then,
With a stifled sob, fell silent again.
'And now,' she shuddered, frowned, and said,
'It's closing time. And I'm for bed.'
She listened a moment, crossed the floor,
And, dumbing on tiptoe—thumb on latch—
The clapper-bell against its catch,
        Stealthily drew wide the door.

All deathly still, the autumnal night
Hung starry and radiant, height to height,
Moon-cold hills and neighbouring wood.

100

Black shadows barred the empty street,
Dew-bright its cobbles at her feet,
And the dead leaves that sprinkled it.
With earthy, sour-sweet smell endued
The keen air coldly touched her skin—
Alone there, at the entering in.
Soon would the early frosts begin,
And the long winter's lassitude,
Mewed up, pent in, companionless.
No light in her mind to soothe and bless;
Only unbridled bitterness
Drummed in her blood against her side.
Her eyelids drooped, and every sense
Languished in secret virulence.
She turned and looked. 'You thought,' she cried,
Small and dull as a toneless bell,
'A silly, country wench like me,
Goose for the fox, befooled could be
By your fine speeches! "Hungry"? Well,
I've been in streets where misery is
Common as wayside blackberries—
Been, and come back; less young than wise.
Go to the parson, knock him up;
He'll dole you texts on which to sup.
Or if his tombstones strike too cold,
Try the old Squire at Biddingfold:
Ask there! He thinks the village pond's
The drink for rogues and vagabonds!'

The Hunter's Moon from a cloudless sky
In pallid splendour earthward yearned;
Dazzling in beauty, cheek and eye:
And her head's gold to silver turned.
Her fierce young face in that wild shine
Showed like a god's, morose, malign.

He rose: and face to face they stood
In sudden, timeless solitude.
The fevered frenzy in her blood
Ebbed, left enfeebled body and limb.
            Appalled, she gazed at him,
Marvelling in horror of stricken heart,
In this strange scrutiny, at what
She saw but comprehended not.
Out of Astarte's borrowed light
She couched her face, to hide from sight
The tears of anguish and bitter pride
That pricked her eyes. 'My God,' she cried,
Pausing in misery on the word,
As if another's voice she had heard,
'Give—if you can—the devil his due—
I'd rather sup with him than you!
So get you gone; no more I want
            Of you, and all your cant!' . . .

A hasty footstep neared; she stayed,
Outwardly bold, but sore afraid.
'Mother!' she mocked. 'Now we shall see
What comes of asking charity.'

Platter in hand, the frugal dame
Back to the counter bustling came.
Something, she saw, had gone amiss.
And one sharp look her daughter's way
Warned her of what she had best not say.
Fearing her tongue and temper, she
Spoke with a smiling asperity.
'Look, now,' she said, 'I've brought you this.
That slut of mine's an hour abed;
The oven chilled, the fire half dead,
The bellows vanished. . . . Well, you have seen

The mort of trouble it has been.
Still, there it is; and food at least.
My husband does not hold with waste;
That's been his maxim all life through.
What's more, it's in the Scriptures too.
By rights we are shut; it's growing late;
And as you can't bring back the plate,
Better eat here—if eat you must!
And now—ah, yes, you'll want a crust.
All this bread is for sale. I'll in
And see what leavings are in the bin.'
Their glances met. Hers winced, and fell;
But why it faltered she could not tell.

The slumbering cat awoke, arose—
Roused by the savour beneath his nose,
Arched his spine, with tail erect,
Stooped, gently sniffing, to inspect
The beggar's feast, gazed after her,
And, seeing her gone, began to purr.
Her daughter then, who had watched the while,
Drew near, and stroked him—with a smile
As sly with blandishment as guile.
Daintily, finger and thumb, she took
A morsel of meat from off the plate,
And with a sidling crafty look
Dangled it over him for a bait:
'No, no; say, please!' The obsequious cat
Reared to his haunches, with folded paws,
Round sea-green eyes, and hook-toothed jaws,
Mewed, snapped, and mouthed it down; and then
Up, like a mannet, sat, begging again.
'Fie, now; he's famished! Another bit?
Mousers by rights should hunt their meat!
That's what the Master says: isn't it?'

The creature fawned on her, and purred,
As if he had pondered every word.
Yet, mute the beggar stood, nor made
A sign he grudged this masquerade.
'I dote on cats,' the wanton said.
'Dogs grovel and cringe at every nod;
Making of man a kind of God!
Beat them or starve them, as you choose,
They crawl to you, whining, and lick your shoes.
Cats know their comfort, drowse and play,
And, when the dark comes, steal away—
Wild to the wild. Make *them* obey!
As soon make water run uphill.
I'm for the night; I crave the dark;
Would wail the louder to hear them bark;
Pleasure myself till the East turns grey.'
She eyed the low window; 'Welladay!
You the greyhound, and I the hare,
I warrant of coursing you'd have your share.
Scrap after scrap she dangled, until
The dainty beast had gorged his fill,
And, lithe as a panther, sheened like silk,
Minced off to find a drink of milk.
'There! That's cat's thanks! His feasting done,
He's off—and half your supper gone! . . .
But, wise or foolish, you'll agree
You had done better to sup with me!'

The stranger gravely raised his head.
'Once was a harvest thick with corn
When I too heard the hunting-horn;
I, too, the baying, and the blood,
And the cries of death none understood.
He that in peace with God would live

Both hunter is and fugitive.
I came to this house to ask for bread,
We give but what we have,' he said;
'Are what grace makes of us, and win
The peace that is our hearts within.'
He ceased, and, yet more gravely, smiled.
'I would that ours were reconciled!'
So sharply intent were sense and ear
On his face and accents, she failed to hear
        The meaning his words conveyed.
"*Peace!*" she mocked him. 'How pretty a jibe!
So jows the death-bell's serenade.
        Try a less easy bribe!'

The entry darkly gaped. And through
The cold night air, a low *a-hoo*,
A-hoo, *a-hoo*, from out the wood,
Broke in upon their solitude;
A call, a bleak decoy, a cry,
Half weird lament, half ribaldry.
She listened, shivered; 'Pah!' whispered she,
'No peace of yours, my God, for me!
I have gone my ways, have eyes, and wits.
Am I a cat to feed on bits
Of dried-up Bible-meat? I know
What kind of bread has that for dough;
Yes, and how honey-sweet the leaven
That starves, on earth, to glut, in heaven!
Dupe was I? Well, come closer, look,
Is my face withered? Sight fall'n in?
Beak-sharp nose and gibbering chin?
Lips that no longer can sing, kiss, pout?
Body dry sinews, the fire gone out?
So it may be with me, Judgment Day,

105

And, men being men, of hope forsook,
Gold all dross—hair gone grey,
Love burnt to ashes.

                  Yet, *still*, I'd say—
Come then, to taunt me, though you may—
I'd treat hypocrites Pilate's way!
False, all false!—Oh, I can see,
You are not what you pretend to be!'

Weeping, she ceased; as flowerlike a thing
As frost ever chilled in an earthly spring.
Mingling moonlight and lamplight played
On raiment and hair; and her beauty arrayed
In a peace profound, as when in glade
On the confines of Eden, unafraid,
Cain and his brother as children strayed.

'What am I saying! I hear it. But none—
None is—God help me!—my own.'

Her mother, listening, had heard
That last low passionate broken word.
What was its meaning? Shame or fear—
It knelled its misery on her ear
       Like voices in a dream.
And, as she brooded, deep in thought,
Trembling, though not with cold, she sought
In her one twinkling candle's beam
From stubborn memory to restore
Where she had seen this man before;
What, in his marred yet tranquil mien—
Dimmed by the veils of time between—
Had conjured the past so quickly back:

Hours when by hopes, proved false, beguiled,
She too had stubborn been and wild,
As vain; but not as lovely. Alas!
And, far from innocent, a child.
A glass hung near the chimney shelf—
She peered into its shadows, moved
By thoughts of one in youth beloved,
Long tongueless in the grave, whom yet
Rancour could shun, but not forget.
Was this blowsed woman here herself?
No answer made the image there—
  Bartered but stare for stare.
She turned aside. What use to brood
On follies gone beyond recall—
Nothing to do the living good,
Secrets now shared by none; and all
Because this chance-come outcast had
Asked for alms a crust of bread.
Clean contrary to common sense,
She'd given him shelter, fetched him food—
Old scraps, maybe, but fit, at worst,
For her goodman; and warmed them first!
And *this* for grace and gratitude!
Charity brings scant recompense
This side of Jordan—from such as he!

But then; what meant that frenzied speech,
Cry of one loved, lost—out of reach,
From girlhood up unheard before,
And past all probing to explore?
What was between them—each with each?
  What in the past lay hid?
Long since the tongue of envy had
Whispered its worst about her child;

Arrogant, beautiful, and wild;
And beauty tarnished may strive in vain
To win its market back again . . .
To what cold furies is life betrayed
When the ashes of youth begin to cool,
When things of impulse are done by rule,
When, sickened of faiths, hopes, charities,
The soul pines only to be at ease;
And—moulting vulture in stony den—
      Waits for the end, Amen!

Thus, in the twinkling of an eye,
This heart-sick reverie swept by;
She must dissemble—if need be—lie;
Rid house and soul of this new pest,
      Prudence would do the rest.
Muffling her purpose, aggrieved in mind.
In she went, and knee on stool,
Deigning no glance at either, leant
Over the tarnished rail of brass
That curtained off the window-glass,
And, with a tug, drew down the blind.
'Lord's Day, to-morrow,' she shrugged. 'No shop!
Come, child, make haste; it's time to sup;
High time to put the shutters up.
The shutters up: *The shutters up*—
Ticked the clock the silence through,
And a yet emptier silence spread.
Shunning the effort, she raised her head;
'And *you'll* be needing to go,' she said.
She seized a loaf, broke off a crust,
Turned, and, 'There's no stale left . . .' began
Coldly, and paused—her haunted eyes
Fixed on the grease-stains, where the cat,

Mumbling its gobbets, had feasting sat.
All doubting gone, pierced to the quick
At hint of this malignant trick,
Like spark in tinder, fire in rick,
A sudden rage consumed her soul
Beyond all caution to control.
Ignored, disdained, deceived, defied!—
'Have you, my God!' she shrilled, 'no pride?
       No shame?
Stranger, you say—and now, a friend!
Cheating and lies, from bad to worse—
Fouling your father's honest name—
Make *me*, you jade, your stalking-horse!
I've watched you, mooning, moping—ay,
       And now, in my teeth, know why!'

A dreadful quiet spread, as when
Over Atlantic wastes of sea,
Black, tempest-swept, there falls a lull,
As sudden as it is momentary,
In the maniac tumult of wind and rain,
Boundless, measureless, monstrous: and then
The insensate din begins again.

      The damsel stirred.
Jade—she had caught the bitter word;
Shame, cheating, lies. Crouched down, she stood,
Lost in a lightless solitude.
No matter; the words were said; all done.
And yet, how strange that this woman should,
Self-blinded, have no heart to see
The secret of her misery;
Should think that she—all refuge gone,
And racked with hatred and shame, could be

The *friend* of this accursèd one!
The anguished blood had left her cheek
White as a leper's. With shaking head,
And eyes insanely wide and bleak,
Her body motionless as the dead,
At bay against a nameless fear,
She strove awhile in vain to speak.
Then, 'Thank you for *that*!' she whispered. 'Who
Brought me into a world like this,
Swarming with evil and deviltries?
Gave me these eyes, this mouth, these feet,
Flesh to hunger—and tainted meat?
Pampered me—flattered—yet taunted me when
Body and soul became prey to men,
And dog to its vomit returned again?
Ask me my name! *You?* Magdalen!
Devils? So be it. What brought me here?—
A stork in the chimney-stack, mother dear?
Oh, this false life! An instant gone
A voice within me said, *See! Have done,
Take to you wings, and, ravening, flee,
Far from this foul hypocrisy!*'
Like an old beldame's her fingers shook,
Mouth puckered, and the inning moon
Gleamed, as she cowered, on brow and eye,
Fixed now in torment on one near by.
'*Friend!* did you say? You heard that? You!—
Forsaken of God, a wandering Jew!
With milk for blood! Speak! Is it true?'

Beyond the threshold a stealthy breeze,
Faint with night's frost-cold fragrances,
         Stirred in the trees.
Ghostlike, on moon-patterned floor there came
A scamper of leaves. The lamp's dim flame

Reared smoking in the sudden draught.
He gazed, but answered not; the Jew.
Woe, beyond mortal eye to trace,
Watched through compassion in his face.
And though—as if the spirit within
Were striving through fleshly bonds to win
Out to its chosen—fiery pangs
Burned in her breast like serpent's fangs,
She lifted her stricken face, and laughed:
Hollowly, ribaldly, *Heugh, heugh, heugh!*
     'A Jew! A Jew!'—
Ran, clawed, clutched up the bread and meat,
     And flung them at his feet.
And then was gone; had taken her flight
Out through the doorway, into the street,
Into the quiet of the night,
On through the moon-chequered shadowy air;
     Away, to where
In woodland of agelong oak and yew,
Echoing its vaulted dingles through,
Faint voices answered her—*Hoo! A-hoo!*
A-hoo! A-hoo!
A-hoo!

A DREAM

Idle I sat—my book upon my knee,
The Tyro's Outline of Biology.
Drowsy the hour: and wits began to roam
Far, far from gene, as far from chromosome.
Sweet sleep stole over me. . . .

                A valley in Spring!—
Wherein a river of water crystal clear
In rarer beauty imaged all things near—
Green grass, and leaf; lithe leopard, swift gazelle—
Gihon? Euphrates? No, I could not tell,
But knew it was Eden by the asphodel,
The painted birds, the songs I heard them sing.

There, where heaven's sunbeams with earth's shade in-
        wove—
This side a slumber-solemn cedar grove,
A clear green twilight underneath a tree,
(Of Life? Of Knowledge? it was strange to me,)
Two mortals sat: a sage, dome-headed, grey,
Who looked a god, albeit in time astray—
Talking, it seemed, his very heart away;
And one even lovelier than woods in May.

She, as if poesy haunted all he said—
Eyes blue as chicory flower, and braided head—
Showed silent as snow against the tender grass,
For naked she as Aphrodite was.
And, at her shoulder, mid its coils near by,
A subtle Serpent couched, with lidless eye,
Which, its tongue flickering, else motionlessly,
Raised its rune-blazoned head, and gazed at me . . .

Whereat, although it harmless seemed, I woke;
My dream-cleansed eyes now fixed upon my book.
Nor could by any stealth I entry win
Into that paradisal scene again—
Fruit so much sweeter to a childish love
Than any knowledge I had vestige of.

A ROSE IN WATER

A rose, in water, to its stem
Decoys a myriad beads of air;
And, lovely with the light on them,
Gives even its thorns their share.

A CHILD ASLEEP

Angel of Words, in vain I have striven with thee,
Nor plead a lifetime's love and loyalty;
Only, with envy, bid thee watch this face,
That says so much, so flawlessly,
And in how small a space!

THE LOOKING-GLASS

'Nothing is so sure that it
May not in a moment flit:
Quench the candle, gone are all
The wavering shadows on the wall.
Eros, like Time, is winged. And, why?
To warn us, dear, he too can fly.
Watch, now, your bright image here
In this water, calm and fair—
Those clear brown eyes, that dark brown hair.
See, I fling a pebble in;
What distortions now begin!
Refluent ripples sweep and sway,
Chasing all I love away.
But, imagine a strange glass
Which, to gaze, gave back, alas,
Nothing but a crystal wall,
And else, no hint of you at all:
No rose on cheek, no red on lip,
No trace of beauty's workmanship.
That, my dear, for me, for you,
Precisely is what life might do.
Might, I say . . . . Oh, then, how sweet
Is it by this stream to sit,
And in its molten mirror see
All that is now reality:
The interlacing boughs, the sun's
Tiny host of flickering moons,
That rainbow kingfisher, and these
Demure, minute anemones—
Cherubim, in heaven's blue,
Leaning their wizard faces too—
Lost in delight at seeing you.'

A POT OF MUSK

A glance—and instantly the small meek flower
Whispered of what it had to childhood meant;
But kept the angel secret of that far hour
      Ere it had lost its scent.

THOMAS HARDY

Mingled the moonlight with daylight—the last in the narrow-
    ing west;
Silence of nightfall lay over the shallowing valleys at rest
      In the Earth's green breast:
Yet a small multitudinous singing, a lully of voices of birds,
Unseen in the vague shelving hollows, welled up with my
    questioning words:
All Dorsetshire's larks for connivance of sweetness seemed
    trysting to greet
Him in whose song the bodings of raven and nightingale meet.

Stooping and smiling, he questioned, 'No birdnotes myself do
    I hear?
Perhaps 'twas the talk of chance farers, abroad in the hush with
    us here—
      In the dusk-light clear?'
And there peered from his eyes, as I listened, a concourse of
    women and men,
Whom his words had made living, long-suffering—they
    flocked to remembrance again;
'O Master,' I cried in my heart, 'lorn thy tidings, grievous thy
    song;
Yet thine, too, this solacing music, as we earthfolk stumble
    along.'

IN A LIBRARY

Would—would that there were
A book on that shelf
To teach an old man
To teach himself!—

The joy of some scribe,
Brush in service to quill,
Who, with bird, flower, landscape,
Emblem and vision,
Loved his margins to fill.

Then might I sit,
By true learning beguiled,
Far into the night
Even with self reconciled,
Retrieving the wisdom
I lost, when a child.

AWAY

There is no sorrow
Time heals never;
No loss, betrayal,
Beyond repair.
Balm for the soul, then,
Though grave shall sever
Lover from loved
And all they share;
See, the sweet sun shines,
The shower is over,
Flowers preen their beauty,
The day how fair!

Brood not too closely
On love, or duty;
Friends long forgotten
May wait you where
Life with death
Brings all to an issue;
None will long mourn for you,
Pray for you, miss you,
Your place left vacant,
You not there.

A PORTRAIT

A solemn plain-faced child stands gazing there,
Her small hand resting on a purple chair.
Her stone-grey waisted gown is looped with black;
Linked chain and star encircle a slender neck;
Knots of bright red deck wrist, breast, flaxen hair;
Shoulder to waist falls band of lettered gold:
Round-eyed, she watches me—this eight-year-old,
The ghost of her father in her placid stare.

Darkness beyond. A moment she and I
Engage in some abstruse small colloquy—
On time, art, beauty, life, mortality!
But of one secret not a hint creeps out—
What grave Velasquez talked to her about;
And from that shadow not a clapper cries
Where now the fowler weaves his subtleties.

AT EASE

Most wounds can Time repair;
　　But some are mortal—these:
For a broken heart there is no balm,
　　No cure for a heart at ease—

At ease, but cold as stone,
　　Though the intellect spin on,
And the feat and practised face may show
　　Naught of the life that is gone;

But smiles, as by habit taught;
　　And sighs, as by custom led;
And the soul within is safe from damnation,
　　　　Since it is dead.

ABSALOM

Vain, proud, rebellious Prince, thy treacherous hair,
Though thirty centuries have come and gone,
Still in that bitter oak doth thee ensnare;
Rings on that broken-hearted, *Son, my son!* . . .

And though, with childhood's tragic gaze, I see
Thee—idol of Israel—helpless in the tree,
Thy dying eyes turned darkened from the Sun;
Yet, of all faces in far memory's shrine—
Paris, Adonis, pale Endymion—
　　The loveliest still is thine.

MEMORY

Ah, Memory—that strange deceiver!
Who can trust her? How believe her—
While she hoards with equal care
The poor and trivial, rich and rare;
Yet flings away, as wantonly,
Grave fact and loveliest fantasy?

When I call her—need her most,
Lo, she's in hiding, or is lost!
Or, capricious as the wind,
Brings stalks—and leaves the flowers behind!
Of all existence—as I live—
She can no more than moments give.
Thousands of dew-clear dusks in Spring
Were mine, time gone, to wander in,
But of their fragrance, music, peace,
What now is left my heart to bless?
Oases in a wilderness!
Nor could her tongue tell o'er the tale
Even of one June nightingale.
And what of the strange world that teems—
Where brooding Hypnos reigns—with dreams?
Twenty years in sleep I have spent—
Horror, delight, grief, wonderment;
Through what wild wizard scenes lured on!
Where are they? . . . In oblivion.
Told she her all, 'twould reach an end
Ere nodded off the drowsiest friend!

She has, it's true, a sovereign skill
A wounded heart to salve and heal;
Can lullaby to sorrow sing;
Shed balm on grief and suffering;

And guard with unremitting care
Secrets that we alone can share.
Ay, so bewitched her amber is
'Twill keep enshrined the tiniest flies—
Instants of childhood, fresh as when
My virgin sense perceived them then—
Daisy or rainbow, a look, a kiss,
As safe as if Eternity's;
And can, with probe as keen, restore
Some fear, or woe, when I was four.
Fleeter than Nereid, plummet-deep,
Enticed by some long-sunken ship,
She, siren-wise, laughs out to see
The treasure she retrieves for me—
Gold foundered when I was a boy,
Now cleansed by Time from all alloy.
And think what priceless boons I owe
Her whimsical punctilio!

Nothing would recognition bring
Should she forsake me. Everything
I will, or want, or plan, or say
Were past conceiving, she away.
Only her exquisite vigilance
Enables me to walk, sing, dance.
Tree and bird would name-less pine
Did she the twain refuse to entwine.
And where, sad dunce, if me she shun,
My A B C? my twice times one?
Fancy her nurseling is; and thought
Can solely in her toils be caught.
Ev'n who and where and what I am
Await her whisper to proclaim.

If only—what the infinite loss!—
I had helped her sever gold from dross!
Since now she is—for better or worse—
The relics of my Universe.
But, ah, how scant a heed she pays
To much well-meaning Conscience says!
And good intentions? Alas for them!
They are left to languish on the stem.
The mort of promises idly made—
Where now their husks, the fickle jade?
Where, too, the jilt so gaily resigned
To out-of-sight being out-of-mind?
And, Love?—I would my heart and she
Were more attuned to constancy!

Musing, she sits, at ease, in peace,
Unchanged by age or time's caprice,
And quietly cons again with me
Some well-loved book of poetry,
Her furtive finger putting by,
With a faint smile, or fainter sigh,
The withered flowers that mark a place
Once over-welled with grief or grace.
Yes, and, as though the wanton tried
Once bitter pangs to gloss, or hide,
She stills a voice fall'n harsh and hoarse
With sudden ill-concealed remorse.
I scan the sphinx-like face, and ask
What still lies hid beneath that mask?—
The sins, the woes, the perfidy—
O murderous taciturnity!
I am the *all* I have ever been,
Why gild the cage thou keep'st me in?
Sweet, sweet! she mocks me, the siren; and then
Its very bars shine bright again.

Yet, of my life, from first to last,
This wayward mistress of the Past—
Soundless foot, and tarn-dark eyes—
Keeps safe for me what most I prize.
The sage may to the Future give
Their *Now*, however fugitive;
Mine savours less of rue and myrrh
When spent, in solitude, with her;
When, kingfisher, on leafy spray,
I while the sunshine hours away
In tranquil joy—as in a dream—
Not of its fish, but of the stream;
Whose gliding waters then reflect
Serener skies, in retrospect,
And flowers, ev'n fairer to the eye
Than those of actuality.

And with what grace she has dealt with me—
What patience, insight, sorcery!
Why, every single word here writ
Was hers, till she surrendered it;
And where, without her—I? for lo,
When she is gone I too must go.

THE REAWAKENING

Green in light are the hills, and a calm wind flowing
    Filleth the void with a flood of the fragrance of Spring;
Wings in this mansion of life are coming and going,
    Voices of unseen loveliness carol and sing.

Coloured with buds of delight the boughs are swaying,
    Beauty walks in the woods, and wherever she rove
Flowers from wintry sleep, her enchantment obeying,
    Stir in the deep of her dream, reawaken to love.

Oh, now begone, sullen care—this light is my seeing;
    I am the palace, and mine are its windows and walls;
Daybreak is come, and life from the darkness of being
    Springs, like a child from the womb, when the lonely
        one calls.

THE SPECTACLE

Scan with calm bloodshot eyes the world around us,
Its broken stones, its sorrows! No voice could tell
The toll of the innocent crucified, weeping and wailing,
In this region of torment ineffable, flame and derision—
        What wonder if we believe no longer in Hell?

        And Heaven? That daybreak vision?
In the peace of our hearts we learn beyond shadow of doubt-
        ing
That our dream of this vanished kingdom lies sleeping within
        us;
Its gates are the light we have seen in the hush of the morning,
When the shafts of the sunrise break in a myriad splendours;
Its shouts of joy are those of all earthly creatures,
Their primal and innocent language—the song of the birds:
Thrush in its rapture, ecstatic wren, and wood-dove tender,
Calling on us poor mortals to put our praise into words.

Passionate, sorrowful hearts, too—the wise, the true and the
        gentle;
Minds that outface all fear, defy despair, remain faithful,
Endure in silence, hope on, assured in their selfless courage,
Natural and sweet in a love no affliction or doubt could dispel.

If, as a glass reflecting its range, we have these for our guidance,
If, as our love creates beauty, we exult in that transient radi-
    ance,
This is the garden of paradise which in our folly
        We abandoned long ages gone.

Though, then, the wondrous divine were ev'n nebulae-distant,
The little we make of our all is our earthly heaven.
        Else we are celled in a darkness,
Windowless, doorless, alone.

LIKE SISTERS

There is a thicket in the wild
By waters deep and dangerous,
Where—close as loveless sisters—grow
Nightshade and the convolvulus.

Tangled and clambering, stalk and stem,
Its tendrils twined against the sun,
The bindweed has a heart-shaped leaf,
Nightshade a triple-pointed one.

The one bears petals pure as snow—
A beauty lingering but a day;
The other's, violet and gold,
Into bright berries shed away;

And these a poisonous juice distil.
Yet both are lovely too—as might
Those rival hostile sisters be:
Different as day is from the night,
When darkness is its dead delight;—
As love is from unchastity.

A RECLUSE

Here lies (where all at peace may be)
A lover of mere privacy.
Graces and gifts were his; now none
Will keep him from oblivion;
How well they served his hidden ends
Ask those who knew him best, his friends.

He is dead; but even among the quick
This world was never his candlestick.
He envied none; he was content
With self-inflicted banishment.
'Let your light shine!' was never his way:
What then remains but, Welladay!

And yet his very silence proved
How much he valued what he loved.
There peered from his hazed, hazel eyes
A self in solitude made wise;
As if within the heart may be
All the soul needs for company:
And, having that in safety there,
Finds its reflection everywhere.

Life's tempests must have waxed and waned:
The deep beneath at peace remained.
Full tides that silent well may be
Mark of no less profound a sea.
Age proved his blessing. It had given
The all that earth implies of heaven;
And found an old man reconciled
To die, as he had lived, a child.

CUPID KEPT IN

When life's wild noisy boys were out of school,
And, for his hour, the usher too was gone,
Peering at sun-fall through the crannied door,
I saw an urchin sitting there alone.

His shining wings lay folded on his back,
Between them hung a quiver, while he sat,
Bare in his beauty, and with poring brows
Bent o'er the saddening task-work he was at.

Which means she?—Yes or No? his problem was.
A gilding ray tinged plume and cheek and chin;
He frowned, he pouted, fidgeted, and wept—
Lost, mazed; unable even to begin!

But then, how could (Oh, think, my dear!), how *could*
That little earnest but unlettered mite
Find any meaning in the heart whose runes
Have kept me tossing through the livelong night?

What wonder, then, when I sighed out for shame,
He brought his scribbled slate, tears in his eyes,
And bade me hide it, until you have made
The question simpler, or himself more wise?

IN THE LOCAL MUSEUM

They stood—rain pelting at window, shrouded sea—
Tenderly hand in hand, too happy to talk;
And there, its amorous eye intent on me,
Plautus impennis, the extinct Great Auk.

THE SCARECROW

In the abandoned orchard—on a pole,
The rain-soaked trappings of that scarecrow have
Usurped the semblance of a man—poor soul—
    Haled from a restless grave.

Geese for his company this fog-bound noon,
He eyeless stares. And I with eyes reply.
Lifting a snakelike head, the gander yelps
    'Ware!' at the passer-by.

It is as though a few bedraggled rags
Poised in this wintry waste were lure enough
To entice some aimless phantom here to mime
    All it is image of . . .

Once Man in grace divine all beauty was;
And of his bone God made a lovelier Eve;
Now even the seraphs sleep at sentry-go;
    The swine break in to thieve

Wind-fallen apples from the two old Trees.
Oh see, Old Adam, once of Eden! Alas!
How is thy beauty fallen: fallen thine Eve,
    Who did all life surpass!

Should in the coming nightfall the Lord God,
Goose-challenged, call, 'My Creature, where art *thou?*'
Scarecrow of hate and vengeance, wrath and blood,
    What would'st thou answer now?

THE BURNING GLASS

No map shows my Jerusalem,
  No history my Christ;
Another language tells of them,
  A hidden evangelist.

Words may create rare images
  Within their narrow bound;
'Twas speechless childhood brought me these,
  As music may, in sound.

Yet not the loveliest song that ever
  Died on the evening air
Could from my inmost heart dissever
  What life had hidden there.

It is the blest reminder of
  What earth in shuddering bliss
Nailed on a cross—that deathless Love—
  Through all the eternities.

I am the Judas whose perfidy
  Sold what no eye hath seen,
The rabble in dark Gethsemane,
  And Mary Magdalene.

To very God who day and night
  Tells me my sands out-run,
I cry in misery infinite,
  'I am thy long-lost son.'

SON OF MAN

(An Epitaph from *Strangers and Pilgrims*)

Son of man, tell me,
Hast thou at any time lain in thick darkness,
Gazing up into a lightless silence,
A dark void vacancy,
Like the woe of the sea
In the unvisited places of the ocean?
And nothing but thine own frail sentience
To prove thee living?
Lost in this affliction of the spirit,
Did'st thou then call upon God
Of his infinite mercy to reveal to thee
Proof of his presence—
His presence and love for thee, exquisite creature of his crea-
	tion?
To show thee but some small devisal
Of his infinite compassion and pity, even though it were as
	fleeting
As the light of a falling star in a dewdrop?
Hast thou? O, if thou hast not,
Do it now; do it now; do it now!
Lest that night come which is sans sense, thought, tongue,
	stir, time, being,
And the moment is for ever denied thee,
Since thou art thyself as I am.

ARROGANCE

I saw bleak Arrogance, with brows of brass,
Clad nape to sole in shimmering foil of lead,
Stark down his nose he stared; a crown of glass
Aping the rainbow, on his tilted head.

His very presence drained the vital air;
He sate erect—stone-cold, self-crucified;
On either side of him an empty chair;
And sawdust trickled from his wounded side.

THE UNRENT PATTERN

I roved the Past—a thousand thousand years,
Ere the Egyptians watched the lotus blow,
Ere yet Man stumbled on his first of words,
Ere yet his laughter rang, or fell his tears;
And on a hillside where three trees would grow—
     Life immortal, Peace, and Woe:
     Dismas, Christ, his bitter foe—
Listened, as yesterday, to the song of birds.

DUST

Sweet sovereign lord of this so pined-for Spring,
How breathe the homage of but one poor heart
With such small compass of thy everything?

Ev'n though I knew this were my life's last hour,
It yet would lie, past hope, beyond my power
One instant of my gratitude to prove,
     My praise, my love.

That 'Everything'!—when this, my human dust,
  Whereto return I must,
Were scant to bring to bloom a single flower!

THE UNUTTERABLE

(September 1940)

What! jibe in ignorance, and scold
The Muses when, the earth in flame,
They hold their peace, and leave untolled
Ev'n Valour's deathless requiem?

Think you a heart in misery,
Riven with pity, dulled with woe,
Could weep in song its threnody,
And to such tombs with chauntings go?

Think you that all-abandoning deeds
Of sacrifice by those whose love
Must barren lie in widow's weeds,
Gone all their youth was dreaming of,

Can be revealed in words? Alas!
No poet yet in Fate's dark count
Has ever watched Night dread as this,
Or seen such evils to surmount.

We stand aghast. Pride, rapture, grief
In storm within; on fire to bless
The daybreak; but yet wiser if
We bide that hour in silentness.

LUCY

Strange—as I sat brooding here,
While memory plied her quiet thread,
Your once-loved face came back, my dear,
    Amid the distant dead.

That pleasant cheek, hair smooth and brown,
Clear brows, and wistful eyes—yet gay:
You stand, in your alpaca·gown,
    And ghost my heart away.

I was a child then; nine years old—
And you a woman. Well, stoop close,
To heed a passion never told
    Under how faded a rose!

Do you remember? Few my pence:
I hoarded them with a miser's care,
And bought you, in passionate innocence,
    A birthday maidenhair.

I see its fronds. Again I sit,
Hunched up in bed, in the dark, alone,
Crazed with those eyes that, memory-lit,
    Now ponder on my own.

You gave me not a thought, 'tis true—
Precocious, silly child; and yet,
Perhaps of all you have loved—loved you,
    I may the last forget.

And though no single word of this
You heed—a lifetime gone—at rest;
I would that all remembrances
    As gently pierced my breast!

A PORTRAIT

Old: yet unchanged;—still pottering in his thoughts
Still eagerly enslaved by books and print;
Less plagued, perhaps, by rigid musts and oughts,
But no less frantic in vain argument;

Still happy as a child, with its small toys,
Over his inkpot and his bits and pieces,—
Life's arduous, fragile and ingenuous joys,
Whose charm failed never—nay, it even increases!

Ev'n happier in watch of bird or flower,
Rainbow in heaven, or bud on thorny spray,
A star-strewn nightfall, and that heart-break hour
Of sleep-drowsed senses between dawn and day;

Loving the light—laved eyes in those wild hues!—
And dryad twilight, and the thronging dark;
A Crusoe ravished by mere solitude—
And silence—edged with music's faintest *Hark!*

And any chance-seen face whose loveliness
Hovers, a mystery, between dream and real;
Things usual yet miraculous that bless
And overwell a heart that still can feel;

Haunted by questions no man answered yet;
Pining to leap from A clean on to Z;
Absorbed by problems which the wise forget;
Avid for fantasy—yet how staid a head!

Senses at daggers with his intellect;
Quick, stupid; vain, retiring; ardent, cold;

Faithful and fickle; rash and circumspect;
And never yet at rest in any fold;

Punctual at meals; a spendthrift, close as Scot;
Rebellious, tractable, childish—long gone grey!
Impatient, volatile, tongue wearying not—
Loose, too: which, yet, thank heaven, was taught to pray;

'Childish' indeed!—a waif on shingle shelf
Fronting the rippled sands, the sun, the sea;
And nought but his marooned precarious self
For questing consciousness and will-to-be;

A feeble venturer—in a world so wide!
So rich in action, daring, cunning, strife!
You'd think, poor soul, he had taken Sloth for bride,—
Unless the imagined is the breath of life;

Unless to speculate bring virgin gold,
And *Let's-pretend* can range the seven seas,
And dreams are not mere tales by idiot told,
And tongueless truth may hide in fantasies;

Unless the alone may their own company find,
And churchyards harbour phantoms 'mid their bones,
And even a daisy may suffice a mind
Whose bindweed can redeem a heap of stones;

Too frail a basket for so many eggs—
Loose-woven: Gosling? cygnet? Laugh or weep?
Or is the cup at richest in its dregs?
The actual realest on the verge of sleep?

One yet how often the prey of doubt and fear,
Of bleak despondence, stark anxiety;
Ardent for what is neither now nor here,
An Orpheus fainting for Eurydice;

Not yet inert, but with a tortured breast
At hint of that bleak gulf—his last farewell;
Pining for peace, assurance, pause and rest,
Yet slave to what he loves past words to tell;

A foolish, fond old man, his bed-time nigh,
Who still at western window stays to win
A transient respite from the latening sky,
And scarce can bear it when the Sun goes in.

THE GNOMON

I cast a shadow. Through the gradual day
Never at rest it secretly steals on;
As must the soul pursue its earthly way
        And then to night be gone.

But Oh, demoniac listeners in the grove,
Think not mere Time I now am telling of.
No. But of light, life, joy, and awe, and love:
        I obey the heavenly Sun.

IZAAK WALTON

That lucent, dewy, rain-sweet prose—
Oh! what a heaven-sent dish
Whereon—a feast for eye, tongue, nose,
Past greediest gourmet's wish—
To serve—not tongues of nightingale,
Not manna soused in hydromel,
Not honey from Hymettus' cell,
Garnished with moly and asphodel—
But Fish!

HENRY VAUGHAN

So true and sweet his music rings,
So radiant is his mind with light
The very intent and meaning of what he sings
May stay half-hidden from sight.

His flowers, waters, children, birds
Lovely as their own archetypes are shown;
Nothing is here uncommon, things or words,
Yet every one's his own.

137

JONATHAN SWIFT

That sovereign mind:
Those bleak, undaunted eyes;
Never to life, or love, resigned—
How strange that he who abhorred cant, humbug, lies,
Should be aggrieved by such simplicities
As age, as ordure, and as size.

SLIM CUNNING HANDS

Slim cunning hands at rest, and cozening eyes—
Under this stone one loved too wildly lies;
How false she was, no granite could declare;
Nor all earth's flowers, how fair.

NO

A drear, wind-weary afternoon,
Drenched with rain was the autumn air;
As weary, too, though not of the wind,
I fell asleep in my chair.

Lost in that slumber I dreamed a dream,
And out of its strangeness in stealth awoke;
No longer alone. Though who was near
I opened not eyes to look;

But stayed for a while in half-heavenly joy,
Half-earthly grief; nor moved:
More conscious, perhaps, than—had she been there—
Of whom,—and how much,—I loved.

138

SEEN AND HEARD

Lovely things these eyes have seen—
Dangling cherries in leaves dark-green;
Ducks as white as winter snow,
Which quacked as they webbed on a-row;
The wren that, with her needle note,
Through blackthorn's foam will flit and float,
    And sun will sheen.

Lovely music my ears have heard—
Catkined twigs in April stirred
By the same air that carries true
Two notes from Africa, *Cuck-oo*;
And then, when night has darkened again,
The lone wail of the willow-wren,
And cricket rasping on, 'Goode'n—goode'n',
    Shriller than mouse or bird.

Ay, and all praise would I, please God, dispose
For but one faint-hued cowslip, one wild rose.

WORDS

Were words sole proof of happiness,
How poor and cold the little I have said!
And if of bitter grief, no less
    Am I discomfited.

The lowliest weed reflects day's noon of light,
Its inmost fragrance squanders on the air;
And a small hidden brook will all the night
    Mourn, beyond speech to share.

139

A SIGN

How shall I know when the end of things is coming?
The dark swifts flitting, the drone-bees humming;
The fly on the window-pane bedazedly strumming;
Ice on the waterbrooks their clear chimes dumbing—
How shall I know that the end of things is coming?

The stars in their stations will shine glamorous in the black;
Emptiness, as ever, haunt the great Star Sack;
And Venus, proud and beautiful, go down to meet the day,
Pale in phosphorescence of the green sea spray—
How shall I know that the end of things is coming?

Head asleep on pillow; the peewits at their crying;
A strange face in dreams to my rapt phantasma sighing;
Silence beyond words of anguished passion;
Or stammering an answer in the tongue's cold fashion—
How shall I know that the end of things is coming?

Haply on strange roads I shall be, the moorland's peace
    around me;
Or counting up a fortune to which Destiny hath bound me;
Or—Vanity of Vanities—the honey of the Fair;
Or a greybeard, lost to memory, on the cobbles in my
    chair—
How shall I know that the end of things is coming?

The drummers will be drumming; the fiddlers at their
    thrumming;
Nuns at their beads; the mummers at their mumming;
Heaven's solemn Seraph stoopt weary o'er his summing;
The palsied fingers plucking, the way-worn feet numbing—
        And the end of things coming.

'IT WAS THE LAST TIME
HE WAS SEEN ALIVE'

'You saw him, then? . . . That very night?'
'A moment only. As I passed by.

The lane goes down into shadow there,
And the sycamore boughs meet overhead;
Then bramble and bracken everywhere,
Moorland, whin, and the wild instead.
But the jasmined house is painted white
        And so reflects the sky.

'He was standing alone in the dwindling dusk,
Close to the window—that rapt, still face,
And hair a faded grey—
Apparently lost in thought; as when
The past seeps into one's mind again,
With its memoried hopes and joys, and pain,
And seduces one back . . .

                        He stirred, and then
Caught sight, it seemed, of the moon in the west—
Like a waif in the heavens astray—
Smiled, as if at her company;
Folded his old hands over his breast;
Bowed: and then went his way.'

FALSE GODS

From gods of other men, fastidious heart,
You thank your stars good sense has set you free.
Ay. But the dread slow piercing of death's dart?
Its, 'Why, *my* God, have I forsaken *thee*.'

INCOMPREHENSIBLE

Engrossed in the day's 'news', I read
Of all in man that's vile and base;
Horrors confounding heart and head—
Massacre, murder, filth, disgrace:
Then paused. And thought did inward tend—
On my own past, and self, to dwell.

Whereat some inmate muttered, 'Friend,
If you and I plain truth must tell,
Everything human we comprehend,
 Only too well, too well!'

THE RUINOUS ABBEY

Stilled the meek glory of thy music;
 Now only the wild linnets sing
Along the confusion of thy ruins,
 And to cold Echo sing.

Quenched the wan purple of thy windows,
 The light-thinned saffron, and the red;
Now only on the sward of thy dominion
 Eve's glittering gold is shed.

Oh, all fair rites of thy religion!—
 Gone now the pomp, the ashen grief;
Lily of Easter, and wax of Christmas;
 Grey water, chrism, and sheaf!

Lift up thy relics to Orion;
 Display thy green attire to the sun;
Forgot thy tombs, forgot thy names and places;
 Thy peace for ever won!

DAY

Wherefore, then, up I went full soon
And gazed upon the stars and moon—
The soundless mansion of the night
Filled with a still and silent light:

And lo! night, stars and moon swept by,
And the great sun streamed up the sky,
Filling the air as with a sea
Of fiery-hued serenity.

Then turned I in, and cried, O soul,
Thank God thine eyes are clear and whole;
Thank God who hath with viewless heaven
Drenched this gross globe, the earth, and given,
In Time's small space, a heart that may
Hold in its span all night, all day!

FRESCOES IN AN OLD CHURCH

Six centuries now have gone
Since, one by one,
These stones were laid,
And in air's vacancy
This beauty made.

They who thus reared them
Their long rest have won;
Ours now this heritage—
To guard, preserve, delight in, brood upon;
And in these transitory fragments scan
The immortal longings in the soul of Man.

THE DUNCE

And 'Science' said,
'Attention, Child, to me!
Have I not taught you all
You touch; taste; hear; and see?

'Nought that's true knowledge now
In print is pent
Which my sole method
Did not circumvent.

'Think you, the amoeba
In its primal slime
Wasted on dreams
Its destiny sublime?

'Yet, when I bid
Your eyes survey the board
Whereon life's How, When, Where
I now record,

'I find them fixed
In daydream; and you sigh;
Or, like a silly sheep,
You bleat me, *Why?*

' "Why is the grass so cool, and fresh, and green?
The sky so deep, and blue?"
Get to your Chemistry,
You dullard, you!

' "Why must I sit at books, and learn, and learn,
Yet long to play?"
Where's your Psychology,
You popinjay?

' "Why stay I here,
Not where my heart would be?"
'Wait, dunce, and ask that
Of Philosophy!

'Reason is yours
Wherewith to con your task;
Not that unanswerable
Questions you should ask.

'Stretch out your hands, then—
Grubby, shallow bowl—
And be refreshed, Child—
Mind, and, maybe, soul!

'Then, when you grow into
A man—like me;
You will as learnéd, wise,
And—happy be!'

ENIGMAS

I weep within; my thoughts are mute
With anguish for poor suffering dust;
Sweet wails the wild bird, groans the brute;
Yet softly to a honied lute
Crieth a voice that heed I must;
    Beckons the hand I trust.

O from nefarious enigmas freed
Shall all that dies not live at last,
Obedient as the seeding weed
Unto fruition come indeed,
    Its perilous blossoming past!

MARTINS

'*Chelidon urbica urbica!*'
I cried on the little bird,
Meticulously enunciating each syllable of each word;
'*Chelidon urbica urbica!*'
Listen to me, I plead!
There are swallows all snug in the hayloft,
I have all that your nestlings can need—
Shadow and sunshine and sweet shallow water—
Come, build in my eaves, and breed!

Fly high, my love! My love, fly low!
I watched the sweet pretty creatures go—
Floating, skimming, and wheeling so
Swiftly and softly—like flakes of snow,
'Gainst the dark of the cedar-boughs, to and fro: . . .
But no!
But no!
'*Chelidon urbica urbica!*'
None paid me the faintest heed.

BLONDIN

With clinging dainty catlike tread,
His pole in balance, hand to hand,
And, softly smiling, into space
He ventures on that threadlike strand.

Above him is the enormous sky,
Beneath, a frenzied torrent roars,
Surging where massed Niagara
Its snow-foamed arc of water pours:

But he, with eye serene as his
Who sits in daydream by the fire,
His every sinew, bone and nerve
Obedient to his least desire,

Treads softly on, with light-drawn breath,
Each inch-long toe, precisely pat,
In inward trust, past wit to probe—
This death-defying acrobat! . . .

Like some old Saint on his old rope-bridge,
Between another world and this,
Dead-calm 'mid inward vortices,
Where little else but danger is.

UNWITTING

This evening to my manuscript
Flitted a tiny fly;
At the wet ink sedately sipped,
Then seemed to put the matter by.
Mindless of him who wrote it, and
His scrutinizing eye—
That any consciousness indeed
Its actions could descry! . . .

Silence; and wavering candlelight;
Night; and a starless sky.

THE CHART

That mute small face, but twelve hours here,
Maps secrets stranger than the sea's,
In hieroglyphics more austere,
And wiser far than Rameses'.

A HARE

Eyes that glass fear, though fear on furtive foot
    Track thee, in slumber bound;
Ears that whist danger, though the wind sigh not,
    Nor Echo list a sound;
Heart—oh, what hazard must thy wild life be,
With sapient Man for thy cold enemy!

Fleet Scatterbrains, thou hast thine hours of peace
    In pastures April-green,
Where the shrill skylark's raptures never cease,
And the clear dew englobes the white moon's beam.
All happiness God gave thee, albeit thy foe
Roves Eden, as did Satan, long ago.

HERE I SIT

Here I sit, and glad am I
So to sit contentedly,
While with never-hastening feet
Time pursues the Infinite;
And a silence centuries-deep
Swathes my mind as if in sleep.
Passive hand, and inward eyes
Press on their transient enterprise;
As, across my paper's white
Creeps the ink from left to right,
Wooing from a soundless brain
The formless into words again:
So I sit, and glad am I
So to sit contentedly.

148

THE 'SATIRE'

The dying man on his pillow
  Turned slowly his head.
'Five years on my Satire on Man
  I spent,' he said.
'But, lying alone, I have mused
  On myself, of late!'

Smiling, he nodded; and glanced
  At the ash in the grate.

COURAGE

O heart, hold thee secure
In this blind hour of stress,
Live on, love on, endure,
Uncowed, though comfortless.

Life's still the wondrous thing
It seemed in bygone peace,
Though woe now jar the string,
And all its music cease.

Even if thine own self have
No haven for defence;
Stand not the unshaken brave
To give thee confidence?

Worse than all worst 'twould be,
If thou, who art thine all,
Shatter ev'n their reality
    In thy poor fall!

AFRAID

Here lies, but seven years old, our little maid,
Once of the darkness Oh, so sore afraid!
Light of the World—remember that small fear,
And when nor moon nor stars do shine, draw near!

THE DREAMER

O thou who giving helm and sword,
  Gav'st too the rusting rain,
And starry dark's all tender dews
    To blunt and stain:

Out of the battle I am sped,
  Unharmed, yet stricken sore;
A living shape amid whispering shades
    On Lethe's shore.

No trophy in my hands I bring,
  To this sad, sighing stream,
The neighings and the trumps and cries
    Were but a dream.

Traitor to life, of life betrayed
  O, of thy mercy deep,
A dream my all, the all I ask
    Is sleep.

THE OLD AUTHOR

The End, he scrawled, and blotted it. Then eyed
Through darkened glass night's cryptic runes o'erhead.
'My last, and longest book.' He frowned; then sighed:
  'And everything left unsaid!'

IX

THE TRAVELLER
[1945]

' "*I saw that the universe is not composed of dead matter but
is . . . a living presence.*" '

'*Le soir vient; et le globe à son tour s'éblouit,
    Devient un oeil énorme et regarde la nuit . . .*

'*Not in lone splendour hung aloft the night
    But watching . . .*'

This Traveller broke at length, toward set of sun,
Out from the gloom of towering forest trees;
Gasped, and drew rein: to gaze, in wonder, down
A bow-shaped gulf of shelving precipices.

The blue of space dreamed level with his eye.
A league beneath, like lava long at rest,
Lay a vast plateau, smooth as porphyry,
Its huge curve gradual as a woman's breast.

In saline marshes Titicaca lies—
Its ruins fabulous ere the Incas reigned:
Was this the like? A mountain sea? His eyes
Watched like a lynx. It still as death remained.

Not the least ripple broke the saffron sheen
Shed by the evening on this wild abyss.
Far countries he had roved, and marvels seen,
But never such a prodigy as this.

No. Water never in a monstrous mass
Rose to a summit like a rounded stone,
Ridged with concentric shadows. No morass
Were vast as this, or coloured zone by zone.

Vague relics haunted him of mythic tales,
Printed in books, or told him in his youth—
Deserts accursed; 'witched islands; sunken bells;
Fissures in space. . . Might one yet prove the truth?

Or, in his own sole being long confined,
Had he been lured into those outskirts where
A secret self is regent; and the mind
Reveals an actual none else can share?—

Prospects enchanting, dread, whereof as yet
No chart has record shown, could bearings tell;
Such as some fabulous Afreet might beget:
Clear as mirage, ev'n less attainable?

Stealthy in onset, between wake and sleep,
Such scenes, more moving than the earth can show,
May, self-created, in mutation sweep,
Silent and fugitive as April snow.

Or had he now attained the true intent
Of his unbroken pilgrimage? The sum
Of all his communings; and what they meant?
Was life at length to its Elysium come?

So flows experience: the vast Without;
Its microcosm, of the Soul, within;
Whereof the day-distracted eye may doubt,
But doubts no more as soon as dreams begin.

Thus mused this Traveller. Was he man or ghost?
Deranged by solitude? Or rapt away
To some unpeopled limbo of the lost—
Feint that the light of morning would betray? . . .

At verge of this huge void he camped for days;
Months of slow journeying from the haunts of men;
Till awe of it no longer could amaze,
And passion for venturing urged him on again.

Down, down into the abysm his mare, on hooves
Nimble as mountain-bred gazelle's, pricked on
From steep to steep, until through bouldered grooves
And shallowing streams she trod, their safety won—

An Arab lean and sleek, her surf-like mane
Tossed on a shoulder as of ivory made;
Full in the moonrise she approached the plain,
Was, with her master, in its beams arrayed.

He had scanned that lunar landscape when of old,
Tranced at a window as a child he had sat—
The Face, the Thorns, those craters grisly cold,
Volcanic seas now parched and desolate;

While from afar the bird of night bewailed
Her cruel ravishment. Even then he had pined,
Ere hope abandoned him, or courage failed,
To seek adventure, safety left behind.

Chilled by his travel in the shrewd clear air,
With wind-strown kindling-wood he built a fire;
Scant pasturage for man or beast was there,
And dreams but transiently assuage desire.

His supper done, he crouched beside the blaze,
Sharp-cheeked, wide-browed, and lost in reverie:
Flamelight and moonshine playing on his face,
The crackle of logs his only company.

When the dark tent of night at daybreak wanned,
He rose, remounted, and surveyed the vast
Convex of bloodshot stone that swept beyond
In arc enormous to the skies at last.

Great mountains he had ranged that lift their snow
In peaks sublime, which age to age remain
Unstirred by foot or voice; but here, a slow
Furtive foreboding crept into his brain

Of what yet lay before him—this Unknown;
In subtle feature so unlike the past
Havens of exile he had made his own,
Been restive in, or wearied of at last.

Soon as the risen sun rilled down its heat,
A dewy mist, in this huge hollow pent,
Washed like a sea of milk his Arab's feet.
And rainbows arched before him as he went.

The call of waters kept his ears a-cock—
Creeks fed by cataracts now left behind.
Forests of fungi in the lichened rock
Showed ashen wan and grey as withy-wind;\

Spawn of a gendering hour, yet hoar with age,
They stood sun-bleached, ephemera of the night,
And—thing past even speculation strange—
Growths never grazed till now by human sight.

What tinier atomies of life were bred
Beneath their skin-thin gills, tents, muted bells,
Eye could not guess—as procreant a bed
As is man's body with its countless cells.

The furtive mist, these clustered funguses—
Minutest stirrings of primeval slime,
The empty heavens, aloof and measureless,
Illusions seemed, not only of space, but time.

From microscopical to the immense—
Mere magnitude of little moment is;
But violent contrast shakes man's confidence
Even in what lies plain before his eyes.

Birds of rare flight and hue, of breed unknown,
Rose, wheeled, fled onward, mewling as they went—
And left him—more forsaken and alone;
Sun for sole guidance in his slow ascent.

But borne not far upon the windless air,
The fickle fleet-winged creatures turned anon;
Came stooping backward on his face to stare:
Broke out in cries again; again, were gone:

Curious, but fearless of what never yet
Had on these mighty slopes been seen to appear;
With soft-tongued jargoning they his way beset,
Sadder than love-lorn pewit's on the ear.

Nor was it only stone that made reply.
Their sweetness echoed in his heart. Delight
And love long pent in fadeless memory
Welled to his eyes. He watched them out of sight.

What meaning harbours in a bird's lone note
Secret as music is; ineffable:
With Song of the Sirens it has been forgot:
But long he journeyed on beneath its spell.

Westward to eastward, wide as gaze could scan,
Shallowly troughed, the void savanna swept:
The dead of all the armies doomed by Man
Might, biding ransom, in its folds have slept.

And, hollow as sinister beating of a drum,
The rock resounded when, with sudden bound,
His beast beneath him, on the treacherous scum,
Slipped, and, with snort of fear, her balance found.

That night, while yet in darkness lapped, it seemed
He had leapt from sleep, that instant made aware
The rock beneath had trembled while he dreamed,
Bleached of a sudden by the lightning's glare.

Foreboding perils unconceived before,
He woke when dawn again suffused the sky.
His earth, once stable, now proved insecure:
He sat and watched it with unwinking eye;

While chattering voices wrangled in his head:
'Alas, what horror of the soul is this?'
'Beware! Away!' 'Far better thou were dead
Than face the ordeal that now before thee lies!'

A plaintive whinny in the early air,
For company calling, solace brought. He smiled.
And in sweet converse with his timorous mare
Soothed her disquiet, and his own beguiled. . . .

Towards noon an arid wind from out the East
Waxed, waned; and failed as they approached—these two,
In close companionship of man and beast,
To where the plain they paced lapsed into blue.

His aching eyes rejoiced. No more there showed
Branched veins of sanguine in a milk-pale stone;
An ever deepening azure gloomed and glowed
In shine and shadow as they journeyed on:

Turquoise, and sapphire, speedwell, columbine.
When clouds minute, like scales of fish, are seen
Dappling an April daybreak, then, divine
As Eros' eyes, there shows a blue between,

Tranquil, wan, infinite. So, pale to dark,
A dark as dazzling as the tropic deep,
Loomed now the prospect toward his distant mark,
When yet again he laid him down to sleep.

In this oblivion he dreamed a dream:—
He dreamed the transitory host of men,
Debased by pride, lust, greed and self-esteem,
Had gone their way; that Earth was freed again.

Their minds had brewed a poison in the blood;
The sap of their own nature had decayed.
They had chosen evil, had resigned the good;
False, faithless, pitiless, and of nought afraid.

Nature, released from this vile incubus,
Had wooed into being creatures of other kind,
Resembling those long since deemed fabulous,
As exquisite in aspect as in mind.

Beings, too, once adored for beauty and grace,
Who had left but echoes in the mirroring air,
Had sought again their bygone dwelling-place;
As happy birds in springtime homeward fare.

And he—the sport of contraries in sleep—
To childhood had returned; gone grief and woe;
That Eden of the heart, and fellowship
With innocence, that only children know;

And in a garden played, serene, alone;
Bird, flower, water, shining in his eyes;
And magic hidd'n in even the tiniest stone . . .
When, suddenly, a Trumpet rent the skies:

To Judgement had been called the Sons of Light,
The stellar host, the Sun and all his brood:
Rank beyond rank, height above heavenly height,
Within the eternal peace of God they stood,

Hymning his glory. And, alas, he knew
That, chosen envoy of the Earth, he had come,
Garbed in her beauty, and enraptured too;
But, though he had yearned for joy, his soul was dumb.

And by unuttered edict exiled thence,
He had fallen, as Satan fell, in leaden dismay,
And thus had wakened to the rock-land whence
His spirit, in fantasy, had winged away. . .

On high a dwindling, sun-bedazzled moon
Paled in the homeless solitudes of space,
Casting gaunt shadow here—his vision gone—
For void companionship in this bitter place.

He, Envoy of the Earth!—that mothering breast;
Those Suns and Sons, what meaning could he find?—
A cold satanic irony at best,
Or scoff of that mocking-bird in sleep, his mind.

Oh, that he had but one bright candle here
To pierce the double-dark of body and soul!
Could but a strain of music reach his ear
To ease this heartsick wretchedness and dole!

From lifted brow his leaden-lidded eyes
Searched the vast furrows of unanswering stone
To where the cedar-arc'd abyss must rise
Whence he had journeyed to this end, alone.

Gazing, he mused, beset by mystery,
Mere Sentience in the silence of the night;
Could Earth itself a living creature be,
And he its transitory parasite?—

A frosted incubus, by the cold congealed,
Doubting his senses, vacantly aware
Of what already instinct had revealed—
His deadliest danger now was blank despair.

Like an old zany, he seemed, who, year by year,
The slave has been of an Excelsior,
Its goal Eureka; and when that draws near
Hears fleshless knuckles on his chamber-door!

Or like a doting lover who at last
By one whose source had seemed of heavenly grace
Forsaken is, in outer darkness cast,
Her cheating blandishment a Lamia's face. . . .

Meagre his saddlebag as camel's hump
When, sand-marooned, she staggers to her doom.
As shrunken too, his Arab's ribs and rump
Showed taut as vellum stretched upon a drum.

He strove in vain to reason, numbed with sleep,
But conscious that at first faint token of dawn,
Wraiths at whose beauty even the blind might weep,
Wooed to his solitude, had come, and gone—

Wraiths all but lost to memory, whose love
Had burned in hearts that never more would beat;
Of whose compassion sense could bring no proof,
Though solace 'twas beyond all telling sweet—

Like flowers that a child brings home; to fade.
Alas, alas, no longing could restore
Life to the faithful by neglect betrayed!
Too late for ransom; they'd return no more—

Had left him, like a castaway adrift,
Lashed to a raft upon a chartless sea,
His only motion the huge roller's lift,
Its depths his only hope at peace to be.

'Sea'! when this waste of stone in which he lay
Like night-blue porcelain was, untinged with red.
But when his cracked lips stirred, as if to pray,
He caught but leaf-dry whisper of what they said.

So tense was this his solitude—the sky
Its mute and viewless canopy—that when
His grieved 'O God!' was followed by a sigh,
It seemed eternity had breathed amen.

Ay, as if cock, horizon-far, had crowed,
His heart, like Peter's, had been rent in twain.
At pang of it his grief again up-flowed,
Though its 'Who's there?' called only in his brain . . .

On, and still on he pressed—scorched heel to nape,
Hunched in his saddle from the noonday's glare—
Watched by a winged thing, high in heaven, agape
To ken aught stirring in a tract so bare,

Which leaf or blade of grass could never yield.
A vitreous region, like a sea asleep,
Crystalline, convex, tideless and congealed,
Profounder far than Tuscarora Deep,

Further than sight could reach, before him lay.
Head bent, eyes fixed—drowsed by recurrent stroke
Of tic-tac ice-like hoof-beats, wits astray,
He slipped again from real to dream: awoke

To find himself marooned beneath a dome
Of star-pricked vacancy, and darkness near;
His breast bespattered with his Arab's foam,
And—trotting at his heels—the spectre, Fear:

Whose fell pursuit, unhastening, pace for pace—
Like Lama of Tibet in waking trance—
His very soul for quarry in the chase,
Forbade all hazard of deliverance:

A shapeless shape of horror, mildew-blue,
With naked feet, blank eyes, and leprous face,
Insane with lust, that ever nearer drew,
Tarrying for midnight and the dread embrace.

Foes of the soul there are, corrupt, malign,
Taint of whose malice is so evil a blight
That ev'n the valiant must hope resign
Unless God's mercy give them means for flight.

Witless as wild bird tangled in a net,
He dared not turn his head, but galloped on,
Spurs red at heel, his body drenched with sweat,
Until, with nerve renewed, but strength nigh gone,

He slowed his pace to listen; gasped, fordone;
Drew rein, dismounted. . . But, the peril past,
His cheek was fallen in like that of one
Whom mortal stroke of fate has felled at last;

And in a moment aged him many years—
Edict beyond the mind to comprehend.
Plaiting cramped fingers in the elf-locked mane,
'Come, now,' he muttered, 'we must rest, my friend.'

The creature's sunken eyeballs, scurfed with rheum
And mute with misery, returned his gaze;
And thus they communed in the gathering gloom,
Nought but the love between them left to graze.

She pawed the unnatural ice, tossed her small head,
By inarticulate alarm distressed;
Baring her teeth, squealed faintly, smitten with dread;
And, snuggling closer, lipped her master's breast.

His breath rasped harshly—wind in blasted wheat;
Through fret of her coarse mane his sun-parched eyes,
Their swol'n lids blackened by the daylong heat,
Swept the dim vacuum of earth and skies.

'Quiet, dear heart! The end is nearing now.
Into disaster thou hast been betrayed.'
He smoothed her gentle muzzle, kissed her brow.
'Nought worse than one more night to live,' he said.

'We both are mortal, both have fallen at last
Into disgrace. But had I swerved aside,
And safety found, what peace, the danger past,
Is his who sleeps with Terror for his bride?

But one night more. And then must come what may.
But never mistress held man's life in fee
As mine has been. And how could speech convey
The woe, forlorn one, that I feel for thee!'

So grieved he in his heart. This comrade dear!
His gentle hand upon her shoulder lay
Though still she shivered, twitching flank and ear,
In this drear wilderness so far astray.

Long stood he motionless, while overhead
The circling constellations, east to west,
Misting the infinite, their effluence shed—
Friends long familiar on how many a quest!

From this dark timeless absence of the mind
It seemed an inward voice had summoned him:—
'See! See!'—a whisper fainter than the wind
Or ripple of water lipped on Lethe's brim.

For now—the zenith darkening—opal-pale,
As if the earth its secret well-spring were—
Softly as flowers of night their scents exhale—
A strange and deepening lustre tinged the air,

Gentle and radiant. So, from off the sea
May mirrored moonbeams, when calm waters lave
A rock-bound coast, steal inward silently,
Blanching the sombre vaultings of a cave.

Not rock his roof-tree here, but hollow sky;
Not reflex moon-ray, but a phantom light,
Like hovering, pervasive reverie
Of Mind supreme, illumining the night.

Rapt in this loveliness, his spellbound face,
To travail the while, and famine, reconciled,
Of fret and weariness shed every trace,
As sleep brings comfort to a tired-out child:

Sleep to a body so pure and exquisite
Like manna it is, at gilding sunrise seen;
The senses so untrammelled that as yet
No more than frailest barrier lies between

Soul and reality. Thus beauty may
Pierce through the mists that worldly commerce brings,
Imagination's blindness wash away,
And—bird at daybreak—lend the spirit wings. . . .

Even the little ant, devoid of fear,
Prowling beneath the shadow of a man,
Conscious may be of occult puissance near,
Whose origin it neither recks, nor can.

So, though he too was now but vaguely aware
Whence welled this boon of benison and peace,
In awe of a mystery so divinely fair,
Tears gushed within him, not of grief but bliss.

Courage revived, like greenness after rain.
Slowly he turned; looked back. And in amaze—
A waif self-exiled from the world of men—
Trembled at sight of what now met his gaze:—

The hushed and visionary host of those
Who, like himself, had faced life's long duress,
Its pangs and horrors, anguish, hardship, woes,
Their one incentive ever on to press,

Defying dread and danger—and in vain:
Not to achieve a merely temporal goal,
Not for bright glory, praise, or greed of gain,
But in that secret craving of the soul

For what no name has; flower of hidden stem:—
The unreturned of kindless land and sea;
Venturers, voyagers, dreamers, seers—ay, them
The Angel of Failure hails with rhapsody. . . .

Him, too, for some rare destiny designed,
Who, in faith and love, has ranged; unmarked, alone;
Though means to share it he will never find
Since its sole language is unique—his own:

Great deeds win sweet renown: the hope forlorn
May perish, and none know what fate it braved;
The self content, at ease, has yet forsworn
The scope that still awaits the soul that's saved:

Faith in a love that can no respite have,
Being its sole resource and anodyne—
Impassioned love, its goal beyond the grave,
However short it fall of the divine.

Ay, even though Man have but one earthly life,
Cradle to grave, wherein to joy and grieve?
His grace were yet the agony and strife
In quest of what no mortal can achieve.

'Angel', forsooth! Bleak visage, frigid breast,
Passionless Nemesis, the heart for prey,
She goads her votary with insane unrest
And smiles upon him when she stoops to slay!

Strange beauty theirs, this host—in rapt array,
Spectral and motionless, intent, and dumb,
Laved in light's loveliness they stretched away
Homage ironic to his Kingdom Come!

Less a mere castaway of flesh and bone,
Defenceless, lost, whom Fate will overwhelm,
He now appeared, than—child of genius—one
Who explores pure fantasy's unbounded realm;

And being at length confronted by ordeal
No human consciousness could comprehend,
A preternatural ecstacy can feel—
Life's kiss of rapture at life's journey's end.

'All hail!' he muttered; paused; then laid him low,
His crazed head pillowed on his Arab's flank;
Prostrate with thirst and weariness and woe,
Into a plumbless deep of sleep he sank.

What visitants of earth or air drew near
Rider and horse in these stark hours of night—
Sylphs of the wilderness or demon drear,
Gazed long and softly, and again took flight,

No sense ajar revealed; nor echo of
Music ethereal, pining sweet and shrill
Of voices in the vaults of heaven above,
The angelic solitudes of Israfel . . .

When daybreak moved above the hushed expanse,
By ague shaken, he awoke. Aware
Nought now could shield him from life's last mischance,
With tranquil mind he breathed the scentless air.

This sterile world!—no weed here raised its head;
No bird on dew-plashed wing, his ear to bless,
Flew up to greet the dayspring; but instead,
A tense unfathomable silentness

Engulfed the enormous convex, stony-still,
Of hueless, lucent crystal where he lay,
Shivering in fever in the sunless chill,
Its centre now scarce half a league away.

He rose; the rustle of his raiment seemed
A desecration of the quietude
Brimming its vacancy; as if there dreamed
A presence here where none had dared intrude

Since waters from waters had divided been,
World from the heavens, the land from ocean freed;
And fruitful trees sprang up, with leafage green,
And earth put forth the herb that yieldeth seed.

'Come, now', he whispered softly; paused; aghast,
Deeming his faithful one had found reprieve;
Had fled away, all tribulation past,
Where even the soul-less languish not nor grieve;

But green-grey willows hang their tresses down;
The heron fishes in his plashy pool;
There, in her beauty floats the silent swan—
Shady and verdurous and calm and cool;

Meadows where asphodel and cowslips blow,
And sunlit summer clouds dissolve in rain—
Her earthly paradise! At length! But no;
The gentle creature heard, had stirred again.

Scrabbling her fore-hoofs on the treacherous waste,
She rose, stood trembling; with sepulchral sigh
Turned her night-blinded eyes, her master faced;
And patiently, piteously set out to die. . . .

To eyried bird above, now rosed with light,
Of insectine dimensions they appeared;
Like emmet creeping, or the weevil-mite
That in a mouldering ship at sea is reared.

Sable in plumage, ruff, and naked head,
Superb in flight, and poised upon his shelf
Of viewless air, he tarried for the dead,
And watched, indifferent as Death himself.

Though the great globe around them grudged them tomb,
Feast they would be for both these ravening foes—
Horseman and Arab, who had dared to roam
Beneath these mountains' never-melting snows.

Halt, maimed and impotent, still travelling on,
O'er very Eye of Earth they made their way,
Till rimmed into the east the risen sun
Flooding its orbit with the joy of day—

That Eye of Heaven, mansion of secret light,
Whose beams of all that's lovely are the shrine,
Procreant, puissant, arbiter of Sight,
Emblem and symbol of the light divine—

So brilliant the least flaw beneath their feet
A tiny shadow cast where nought there was
Taller than locust in the rilling heat
To check the splendour of this sea of glass.

And if pure radiance could pure music be,
And quiet supreme its tabernacle were,
This orb, now blazing in its majesty,
With a sublime Hosanna rent the air.

Moved by an impulse beyond wit to scan,
His poor rags stirring in a fitful breeze,
This worn, outwearied, errant son of man
Paused, bowed his head, fell down upon his knees;

And, with a faint and lamentable cry,
Poured hoarsely forth a babble of praise and prayer,
Sun on his brows, above the boundless sky,
No living soul to hear or heed him there . . .

A self there is that listens in the heart
To what is past the range of human speech,
Which yet has urgent tidings to impart—
The all-but-uttered, and yet out of reach.

Beneath him an immeasurable well
Of lustrous crystal motionlessly black
Deeped on. And as he gazed—marvel past words to tell—
It seemed to him a presence there gazed back:

Rapt, immaterial, remote; ev'n less
In substance than is image of the mind;
And yet, in all-embracing consciousness
Of its own inmost being; elsewise blind:

Past human understanding to conceive;
Of virgin innocence, yet source of all
That matter had the power to achieve
Ere Man created was, ere Adam's fall:

And in its midst a mote scarce visible—
Himself: the momentary looking-glass
Of Nature, which a moment may annul,
And with earth's hosts may into nothing pass:

The flux of change. Ay, this poor Traveller too—
Soon to be dust, though once erect, elate,
From whose clear gaze a flame divine burned through;
A son of God—no sport of Time or Fate:

It seemed his heart was broken; his whole life long
Concentrated in this moment of desire;
Its woe, its rapture, transient as the song
The Phoenix sings upon her funeral pyre.

'Alas', he gasped—his journey now at end;
Breathed softly out his last of many sighs;
Flung forth his hands, and motionless remained,
Drenched through with day; and darkness in his eyes . . .

Head drooped, knees sagging, his forsaken jade—
Her stark hide gilded by the eastern sun,
Her abject carcass in its glory arrayed—
As though in fear to break his prayers, drowsed on.

But, as an acid frets its way through steel,
Into her sentience at length there crept
A deeper hush no silence could conceal—
And Death for long has never secret kept,

Though shadow-close it mime its sister, Sleep,
The creature nearer drew—reluctant, slow,
As if, like motherless child, to sigh and weep,
Too young the import of its loss to know.

Ears pricked, reins dangling, thus a while she stayed—
Of that in watch above full well aware:
'See, now, dear master, here I wait!' She neighed,
And stooping, snuffed the rags, the matted hair;

Then, of a sudden, in panic dread, upreared,
Plunged, wheeled, drew back, her eyeballs gleaming white,
And urged to frenzy by the thing she feared
From all that love had left on earth took flight . . .

Sweet is that Earth, though sorrow and woe it have,
Though parched, at length, the milk within its breast;
And then the night-tide of the all-welcoming grave
For those who weary, and a respite crave:
Inn at the cross roads, and the traveller's rest . . .

X

O LOVELY ENGLAND

[1953]

O LOVELY ENGLAND

O lovely England, whose ancient peace
    The direst dangers fret,
Be on the memory of your past
    Your sure devotion set;
Give still true freedom to fulfil,
    Your all without regret!

Heed, through the troubles that benumb
    Voices now stilled, yet clear,
Chaunting their deathless songs—too oft
    To ears that would not hear;
Urging you, solemn, sweet, to meet
    Your fate unmoved by fear.

Earth's ardent life incites you yet
    Beyond the encircling seas;
And calls to causes else forlorn,
    The children at your knees:
May their brave hearts in days to come
    Dream unashamed of these!

". . . ALL GONE . . ."

'Age takes in pitiless hands
All one loves most away;
Peace, joy, simplicity—
Where then their inward stay?'—

Or so, at least they say.

'Marvel of noontide light,
Of gradual break of day;
Dreams, visions of the night
Age withers all away.'—

Yes, that is what they say.

'Wonder of winter snow,
Magic of wandering moon,
The starry hosts of heaven—
Come seventy, all are gone.

'Unhappy when alone,
Nowhere at peace to be;
Drowned the old self-sown eager thoughts
Constantly stirring in thee!' . . .

Extraordinary!
That's what they *say* to me!

WE WHO HAVE *WATCHED*

We who have watched the World go by,
Brooding with eyes, unveiled and clear,
On its poor pomp and vanity,
Seen Mammon, vice and infamy
Cringe, bargain, jape and jeer—
What surety have we here?

We who have witnessed beauty fade,
And faces once divine with light
In narrow abject darkness laid,
Consigned with busy heedless spade
To clay from mortal sound and sight—
Where look we for delight?

We who have seen the tender child
Leap from its mother's breast, to rove
This earth; and soon, by fiend beguiled,
With wanton sickliness defiled,
Resign at last faith, hope and love.

What mercy dream *we* of?

THE BOURNE

Rebellious heart, why still regret so much
A destiny which all that's mortal shares?
Surely the solace of the grave is such
That there naught matters; and, there, no one cares?

Nor faith, nor love, nor dread, nor closest friend
Can from this nearing bourne your footfall keep:
But there even conflict with your self shall end,
And every grief be reconciled in Sleep.

DE PROFUNDIS

The metallic weight of iron;
The glaze of glass;
The inflammability of wood . . .

You will not be cold there;
You will not wish to see your face in a mirror;
There will be no heaviness,
Since you will not be able to lift a finger.

There will be company, but they will not heed you;
Yours will be a journey only of two paces
Into view of the stars again; but you will not make
    it.

There will be no recognition;
No one, who should see you, will say—
Throughout the uncountable hours—

'Why . . . the last time we met. I brought you some
    flowers!'

WHEN LOVE FLIES IN

When Love flies in,
Make—make no sign;
Owl-soft his wings,
Sand-blind his eyne;
Sigh, if thou must,
But seal him thine.

Nor make no sign
If love flit out;
He'll tire of thee
Without a doubt.
Stifle thy pangs;
Thy heart resign;
And live without!

RHYMES AND VERSES

NICHOLAS NYE

Thistle and darnel and dock grew there,
  And a bush, in the corner, of may;
On the orchard wall I used to sprawl
  In the blazing heat of the day;
Half asleep and half awake,
  While the birds went twittering by,
And nobody there my lone to share
    But Nicholas Nye.

Nicholas Nye was lean and grey,
  Lame of a leg and old,
More than a score of donkey's years
  He had seen since he was foaled;
He munched the thistles, purple and spiked,
  Would sometimes stoop and sigh,
And turn his head, as if he said,
    'Poor Nicholas Nye!'

Alone with his shadow he'd drowse in the meadow
  Lazily swinging his tail,
At break of day he used to bray,—
  Not much too hearty and hale;

But a wonderful gumption was under his skin,
   And a clear calm light in his eye,
And once in a while: he'd smile . . .
     Would Nicholas Nye.

Seem to be smiling at me, he would,
   From his bush in the corner, of may,—
Bony and ownerless, widowed and worn,
   Knobble-kneed, lonely and grey;
And over the grass would seem to pass
   'Neath the deep dark blue of the sky,
Something much better than words between me
     And Nicholas Nye.

But dusk would come in the apple boughs,
   The green of the glow-worm shine,
The birds in nest would crouch to rest,
   And home I'd trudge to mine;
And there, in the moonlight, dark with dew,
   Asking not wherefore nor why,
Would brood like a ghost, and as still as a post.
     Old Nicholas Nye.

ECHOES

The sea laments
The livelong day,
Fringing its waste of sand;
Cries back the wind from the whispering shore—
No words I understand:
Yet echoes in my heart a voice,
As far, as near, as these—
The wind that weeps,
The solemn surge
Of strange and lonely seas.

'I DREAM OF A PLACE'

I dream of a place where I long to live always:
Green hills, shallow sand dunes, and nearing the sea;

The house is of stone; there are twelve lattice windows,
And a door, with a keyhole—though lost is the key.

Thick-thatched is the roof; it has low, white-washed chimneys,
Where doves preen their wings, and coo, *Please*, love; love *me!*

There martins are flitting; the sun shines; the moon shines;
Drifts of bright flowers are adrone with the bee;

And a wonderful music of bird-song at daybreak
Wells up from the bosom of every tree.

A brook of clear water encircles the garden,
With kingcups, and cress, and the white *fleur de lys*—

Moorhens and dabchicks; the wild duck at evening
Wing away to the sun, in the shape of a V;

And the night shows the stars, shining in at the windows,
Brings nearer the far-away sigh of the sea.

Oh, the quiet, the green of the grass, the grey willows,
The light, and the shine, and the air sweet and free!—

That dream of a place where I long to live always:
Low hills, shallow sand dunes—at peace there to be!

TREES

Of all the trees in England,
  Her sweet three corners in,
Only the Ash, the bonnie Ash
  Burns fierce while it is green.

Of all the trees in England,
  From sea to sea again,
The Willow loveliest stoops her boughs
  Beneath the driving rain.

Of all the trees in England,
  Past frankincense and myrrh,
There's none for smell, of bloom and smoke,
  Like Lime and Juniper.

Of all the trees in England,
  Oak, Elder, Elm and Thorn,
The Yew alone burns lamps of peace
  For them that lie forlorn.

THE HOLLY

The sturdiest of forest-trees
With acorns is inset;
Wan white blossoms the elder brings
To fruit as black as jet;
But O, in all green English woods
Is aught so fair to view
As the sleek, sharp, dark-leaved holly tree
And its berries burning through?

Towers the ash; and dazzling green
The larch her tassels wears;
Wondrous sweet are the clots of may
The tangled hawthorn bears;
But O, in heath or meadow or wold
Springs aught beneath the blue
As brisk and trim as a holly-tree bole
With its berries burning through?

When hither, thither, falls the snow,
And blazes small the frost,
Naked amid the winter stars
The elm's vast boughs are tossed;
But O, of all that summer showed
What now to winter's true
As the prickle-beribbed dark holly tree,
With its berries burning through!

BUNCHES OF GRAPES

'Bunches of grapes,' says Timothy;
'Pomegranates pink,' says Elaine;
'A junket of cream and a cranberry tart
    For me,' says Jane.

'Love-in-a-mist,' says Timothy;
'Primroses pale,' says Elaine;
'A nosegay of pinks and mignonette
    For me,' says Jane.

Chariots of gold,' says Timothy;
'Silvery wings,' says Elaine;
'A bumpity ride in a wagon of hay
    For me,' says Jane.

TARTARY

If I were Lord of Tartary,
  Myself, and me alone,
My bed should be of ivory,
  Of beaten gold my throne;
And in my court should peacocks flaunt,
And in my forests tigers haunt,
And in my pools great fishes slant
    Their fins athwart the sun.

If I were Lord of Tartary,
  Trumpeters every day
To all my meals should summon me,
  And in my courtyards bray;
And in the evening lamps should shine,
Yellow as honey, red as wine,
While harp, and flute, and mandoline
    Made music sweet and gay.

If I were Lord of Tartary,
  I'd wear a robe of beads,
White, and gold, and green they'd be—
  And small and thick as seeds;
And ere should wane the morning star,
I'd don my robe and scimitar,
And zebras seven should draw my car
    Through Tartary's dark glades.

Lord of the fruits of Tartary,
  Her rivers silver-pale!
Lord of the hills of Tartary,
  Glen, thicket, wood, and dale!

Her flashing stars, her scented breeze,
Her trembling lakes, like foamless seas,
Her bird-delighting citron-trees,
  In every purple vale!

KING DAVID

King David was a sorrowful man:
  No cause for his sorrow had he:
And he called for the music of a hundred harps,
  To solace his melancholy.

They played till they all fell silent:
  Played—and play sweet did they;
But the sorrow that haunted the heart of King David
  They could not charm away.

He rose; and in his garden
  Walked by the moon alone,
A nightingale hidden in a cypress-tree
  Jargoned on and on.

King David lifted his sad eyes
  Into the dark-boughed tree—
'Tell me, thou little bird that singest,
  Who taught my grief to thee?'

But the bird in no wise heeded;
  And the king in the cool of the moon
Hearkened to the nightingale's sorrowfulness,
  Till all his own was gone.

NOT I

As I came out of Wiseman's Street,
The air was thick with driven sleet;
Crossing over Proudman's Square
Cold louring clouds obscured the air;
But as I entered Goodman's Lane
The burning sun came out again;
And on the roofs of Children's Row
In solemn glory shone the snow.

UNDER THE ROSE
(*The Song of the Wanderer*)

Nobody, nobody told me
What nobody, nobody knows:
But now I know where the Rainbow ends,
I know where there grows
A Tree that's called the Tree of Life,
I know where there flows
The River of All-Forgottenness,
And where the Lotus blows,
And I—I've trodden the forest, where
In flames of gold and rose,
To burn, and then arise again,
   The Phoenix goes.

Nobody, nobody told me
What nobody, nobody knows;
Hide thy face in a veil of light,
Put on thy silver shoes,

184

Thou art the Stranger I know best,
Thou art the sweet heart, who
Came from the Land between Wake and Dream,
Cold with the morning dew.

THE DOUBLE

I curtseyed to the dovecote.
I curtseyed to the well.
I twirled me round and round about,
The morning scents to smell.
When out I came from spinning so,
Lo, betwixt green and blue
Was the ghost of me—a fairy child—
A-dancing—dancing, too.

Nought was of her wearing
That is the earth's array.
Her thistledown feet beat airy fleet,
Yet set no blade astray.
The gossamer shining dews of June
Showed grey against the green;
Yet never so much as a bird's-claw print
Of footfall to be seen.

Fading in the mounting sun,
That image soon did pine.
Fainter than moonlight thinned the locks
That shone as clear as mine.
Vanished! Vanished! O, sad it is
To spin and spin—in vain;
And never to see the ghost of me
A-dancing there again.

SONG

O for a moon to light me home!
  O for a lanthorn green!
For those sweet stars the Pleiades,
That glitter in the twilight trees;
  O for a lovelorn taper! O
  For a lanthorn green!

O for a frock of tartan!
  O for clear, wild, grey eyes!
For fingers light as violets,
'Neath branches that the blackbird frets;
  O for a thistly meadow! O
  For clear, wild, grey eyes!

O for a heart like almond boughs!
  O for sweet thoughts like rain!
O for first-love like fields of grey,
Shut April-buds at break of day!
  O for a sleep like music!
  Dreams still as rain!

THE SONG OF THE MAD PRINCE

Who said, 'Peacock Pie'?
  The old King to the sparrow:
Who said, 'Crops are ripe'?
  Rust to the harrow:
Who said, 'Where sleeps she now?
Where rests she now her head,
Bathed in eve's loveliness'?—
  That's what I said.

Who said, 'Ay, mum's the word';
    Sexton to willow:
Who said, 'Green dusk for dreams,
    Moss for a pillow'?
Who said, 'All Time's delight
    Hath she for narrow bed;
Life's troubled bubble broken'?—
    That's what I said.

THE SONG OF SHADOWS

Sweep thy faint strings, Musician,
    With thy long lean hand;
Downward the starry tapers burn,
    Sinks soft the waning sand;
The old hound whimpers couched in sleep,
    The embers smoulder low;
Across the walls the shadows
        Come, and go.

Sweep softly thy strings, Musician,
    The minutes mount to hours;
Frost on the windless casement weaves
    A labyrinth of flowers;
Ghosts linger in the darkening air,
    Hearken at the open door;
Music hath called them, dreaming,
        Home once more.

I MET AT EVE

I met at eve the Prince of Sleep,
His was a still and lovely face,
He wandered through a valley steep,
　　Lovely in a lonely place.

His garb was grey of lavender,
About his brows a poppy-wreath
Burned like dim coals, and everywhere
　　The air was sweeter for his breath.

His twilight feet no sandals wore,
His eyes shone faint in their own flame,
Fair moths that gloomed his steps before
　　Seemed letters of his lovely name.

His house is in the mountain ways,
A phantom house of misty walls,
Whose golden flocks at evening graze,
　　And 'witch the moon with muffled calls.

Upwelling from his shadowy springs
Sweet waters shake a trembling sound,
There flit the hoot-owl's silent wings,
　　There hath his web the silkworm wound.

Dark in his pools clear visions lurk,
And rosy, as with morning buds,
Along his dales of broom and birk
　　Dreams haunt his solitary woods.

I met at eve the Prince of Sleep,
His was a still and lovely face,
He wandered through a valley steep,
　　Lovely in a lonely place.

PRECIOUS STONES

Ruby, amethyst, emerald, diamond,
Sapphire, sardonyx, fiery-eyed carbuncle,
    Jacynth, jasper, crystal a-sheen;
Topaz, turquoise, tourmaline, opal,
    Beryl, onyx and aquamarine:—
Marvel, O mortal!—their hue, lustre, loveliness,
Pure as a flower when its petals unfurl—
Peach-red carnelian, apple-green chrysoprase,
    Amber and coral and orient pearl!

STARS

If to the heavens you lift your eyes
  When Winter reigns o'er our Northern skies,
  And snow-cloud none the zenith mars,
  At Yule-tide midnight these your stars:
Low in the South see bleak-blazing Sirius;
Above him hang Betelgeuse, Procyon wan;
Wild-eyed to West of him, Rigel and Bellatrix,
And rudd-red Aldebaran journeying on.
High in night's roof-tree beams twinkling Capella;
Vega and Deneb prowl low in the North;
Far to the East roves the Lion-heart, Regulus;
While the twin sons of Zeus to'rd the zenith gleam forth.

But when Midsummer Eve in man's sleep-drowsed hours
Refreshes for daybreak its dew-bright flowers,
Though three of these Night Lights aloft remain,
For nine, if you gaze, you will gaze in vain.
Yet comfort find, for, far-shining there,
See golden Arcturus and cold Altaïr;
Crystalline Spica, and, strange to scan,
Blood-red Antares, foe to Man.

SILVER

Slowly, silently, now the moon
Walks the night in her silver shoon;
This way, and that, she peers, and sees
Silver fruit upon silver trees;
One by one the casements catch
Her beams beneath the silvery thatch;
Couched in his kennel, like a log,
With paws of silver sleeps the dog;
From their shadowy cote the white breasts peep
Of doves in a silver-feathered sleep;
A harvest mouse goes scampering by,
With silver claws, and silver eye;
And moveless fish in the water gleam,
By silver reeds in a silver stream.

THE MOTHER BIRD

Through the green twilight of a hedge
I peered, with cheek on the cool leaves pressed,
And spied a bird upon a nest:
Two eyes she had beseeching me
Meekly and brave, and her brown breast
Throbb'd hot and quick above her heart;
And then she opened her dagger bill,—
'Twas not the chirp that sparrows pipe
At early day; 'twas not the trill,
That falters through the quiet even;
But one sharp solitary note,
One desperate fierce and vivid cry
Of valiant tears, and hopeless joy,
One passionate note of victory.
Off, like a fool afraid, I sneaked,
Smiling the smile the fool smiles best,

At the mother bird in the secret hedge
Patient upon her lonely nest.

THE OLD SAILOR

There came an old sailor
Who sat to sup
Under the trees
Of the *Golden Cup*.

Beer in a mug
And a slice of cheese
With a hunk of bread
He munched at his ease.

Then in the summer
Dusk he lit
A little black pipe,
And sucked at it.

He thought of his victuals,
Of ships, the sea,
Of his home in the West,
And his children three.

And he stared and stared
To where, afar,
The lighthouse gleamed
At the harbour bar;

Till his pipe grew cold,
And down on the board
He laid his head,
And snored, snored, snored.

KINGS

King Canute
　　Sat down by the sea,
Up washed the tide
　　And away went he.

Good King Alfred
　　Cried, 'My sakes!
Not five winks,
　　And look at those cakes!'

Lackland John
　　Were a right royal Tartar
Till he made his mark
　　Upon *Magna Carta:*

Ink, seal, table,
　　On Runnymede green,
Anno Domini
　　12 — 15

BABEL

The sea washes England,
Where all men speak
A language rich
As ancient Greek.

The wide world over
Man with man
Has talked his own tongue
Since speech began.

Yet still must sorrow
Move the mind.

He understands
But his own kind.

The voices lovely,
Hollow, drear,
Of beast and bird
Beat on his ear:

Eye into eye
Gaze deep he may;
Yet still through Babel
Gropes his way.

JOHN MOULDY

I spied John Mouldy in his cellar,
Deep down twenty steps of stone;
In the dusk he sat a-smiling,
    Smiling there alone.

He read no book, he snuffed no candle;
The rats ran in, the rats ran out;
And far and near, the drip of water
    Went whisp'ring about.

The dusk was still, with dew a-falling,
I saw the Dog-star bleak and grim,
I saw a slim brown rat of Norway
    Creep over him.

I spied John Mouldy in his cellar,
Deep down twenty steps of stone;
In the dusk he sat a-smiling,
    Smiling there alone.

THE SILVER PENNY

'Sailorman, I'll give to you
   My bright silver penny,
If out to sea you'll sail me
   And my dear sister Jenny.'

'Get in, young sir, I'll sail ye
   And your dear sister Jenny,
But pay she shall her golden locks
   Instead of your penny.'

They sail away, they sail away,
   O fierce the winds blew!
The foam flew in clouds
   And dark the night grew!

And all the green sea-water
   Climbed steep into the boat;
Back to the shore again
   Sail they will not.

Drowned is the sailorman,
   Drowned is sweet Jenny,
And drowned in the deep sea
   A bright silver penny.

HI!

Hi! handsome hunting man
Fire your little gun.
Bang! Now the animal
Is dead and dumb and done.
Nevermore to peep again, creep again, leap again,
Eat or sleep or drink again, Oh, what fun!

MARCHING SONG

Far away in Nanga-noon
Lived an old and grey Baboon,
Ah-mi, Sulâni!
Once a Prince among his kind,
Now forsaken, left behind,
Feebly, lonely, all but blind:
Sulâni, ghar magleer.

Peaceful Tishnar came by night,
In the moonbeams cold and white;
Ah-mi, Sulâni!
'Far away from Nanga-noon,
Old and lonely, gray Baboon;
Is a journey for thee soon!
Sulâni, ghar magleer.

'Be not frightened, shut thine eye;
Comfort take, nor weep, nor sigh;
Solitary Tishnar's nigh!'
Sulâni, ghar magleer.

Old Baboon, he gravely did
All that peaceful Tishnar bid;
Ah-mi, Sulâni!
In the darkness cold and grim
Drew his blanket over him;
Closed his old eyes, sad and dim:
Sulâni, ghar magleer.

Talaheeti sul magloon
Olgar, ulgar Manga–noon;
Ah–mi Sulâni!
Tishnar sootli maltmahee,
Ganganareez soongalee,
Manni Mulgar sang suwhee
Sulâni, ghar magleer.

[From *The Three Royal Monkeys*]

THE WATER MIDDEN'S SONG

Bubble, Bubble,
Swim to see
Oh, how beautiful
I be.

Fishes, Fishes,
Finned and fine,
What's your gold
Compared with mine?

Why, then, has
Wise Tishnar made
One so lovely
One so sad?

Lone am I,
And can but make
A little song,
For singing's sake.

ALL BUT BLIND

All but blind
  In his chambered hole
Gropes for worms
  The four-clawed Mole.

All but blind
  In the evening sky
The hooded Bat
  Twirls softly by.

All but blind
  In the burning day
The Barn-Owl blunders
  On her way.

And blind as are
  These three to me,
So, blind to Some-One
  I must be.

OFF THE GROUND

Three jolly Farmers
Once bet a pound
Each dance the others would
Off the ground.

Out of their coats
They slipped right soon,
And neat and nicesome,
Put each his shoon.

One—Two—Three!—
And away they go,
Not too fast,
And not too slow:
Out from the elm-tree's
Noonday shadow,
Into the sun
And across the meadow.
Past the schoolroom,
With knees well bent
Fingers a-flicking,
They dancing went.
Up sides and over,
And round and round,
They crossed click-clacking,
The Parish bound.
By Tupman's meadow
They did their mile,
Tee-to-tum
On a three-barred stile.
Then straight through Whipham,
Downhill to Week,
Footing it lightsome,
But not too quick,
Up fields to Watchet,
And on through Wye,
Till seven fine churches
They'd seen skip by—
Seven fine churches,
And five old mills,
Farms in the valley,
And sheep on the hills;
Old Man's Acre
And Dead Man's Pool

All left behind,
As they danced through Wool.

And Wool gone by,
Like tops that seem
To spin in sleep
They danced in dream:
Withy—Wellover—
Wassop—Wo—
Like an old clock
Their heels did go.
A league and a league
And a league they went,
And not one weary,
And not one spent.
And lo, and behold!
Past Willow-cum-Leigh
Stretched with its waters
The great green sea.

Says Farmer Bates,
'I puffs and I blows,
What's under the water,
Why, no man knows!'
Says Farmer Giles,
'My wind comes weak,
And a good man drownded
Is far to seek'.
But Farmer Turvey,
On twirling toes
Up's with his gaiters,
And in he goes:
Down where the mermaids
Pluck and play

On their twangling harps
In a sea-green day;
Down where the mermaids,
Finned and fair,
Sleek with their combs
Their yellow hair. . . .

Bates and Giles—
On the shingle sat,
Gazing at Turvey's
Floating hat.
But never a ripple
Nor bubble told
Where he was supping
Off plates of gold.
Never an echo
Rilled through the sea
Of the feasting and dancing
And minstrelsy.
They called—called—called:
Came no reply:
Nought but the ripples'
Sandy sigh.
Then glum and silent
They sat instead,
Vacantly brooding
On home and bed,
Till both together
Stood up and said:—
'Us knows not, dreams not,
Where you be,
Turvey, unless
In the deep blue sea;
But axcusing silver—

And it comes most willing—
Here's us two paying
Our forty shilling;
For it's sartin sure, Turvey,
Safe and sound,
You danced us square, Turvey;
Off the ground!'

THE ENGLISHMAN

I met a sailor in the woods,
  A silver ring wore he,
His hair hung black, his eyes shone blue.
  And thus he said to me:—

'What country, say, of this round earth,
  What shore of what salt sea,
Be this, my son, I wander in,
  And looks so strange to me?'

Says I, 'O foreign sailorman,
  In England now you be,
This is her wood, and there her sky,
  And that her roaring sea.'

He lifts his voice yet louder,
  'What smell be this,' says he
'My nose on the sharp morning air
  Snuffs up so greedily?'

Says I, 'It is wild roses
  Do smell so winsomely,
And winy briar too,' says I,
  'That in these thickets be.'

'And oh!' says he, 'what leetle bird
   Is singing in yon high tree,
So every shrill and long-drawn note
   Like bubbles breaks in me?'

Says I, 'It is the mavis
   That perches in the tree,
And sings so shrill, and sings so sweet,
   When dawn comes up the sea.'

At which he fell a-musing,
   And fixed his eye on me,
As one alone 'twixt light and dark
   A spirit thinks to see.

'England!' he whispers soft and harsh,
   'England!' repeated he,
'And briar, and rose, and mavis,
   A-singing in yon high tree.

'Ye speak me true, my leetle son,
   So—so, it came to me,
A-drifting landwards on a spar,
   And grey dawn on the sea.

'Ay, ay, I could not be mistook;
   I knew them leafy trees,
I knew that land so witchery sweet,
   And that old noise of seas.

'Though here I've sailed a score of years,
   And heard 'em, dream or wake,
Lap small and hollow 'gainst my cheek,
   On sand and coral break:

' "Yet now," my leetle son, says I,
    A-drifting on the wave,
"That land I see so safe and green
    Is England, I believe.

' "And that there wood is English wood,
    And this here cruel sea,
The selfsame old blue ocean
    Years gone remembers me,

' "A-sitting with my bread and butter
    Down behind yon chitterin' mill;
And this same Marinere"—(that's me),
"Is that same leetle Will!—

' "That very same wee leetle Will
    Eating his bread and butter there,
A-looking on the broad blue sea
    Betwixt his yaller hair!"

'And here be I, my son, throwed up
    Like corpses from the sea,
Ships, stars, winds, tempests, pirates past,
    Yet leetle Will I be!'

He said no more, that sailorman,
    But in a reverie
Stared like the figure of a ship
    With painted eyes to sea.

INDEX OF FIRST LINES